Guilt-Free Motherhood

How to Raise Great Kids & Have Fun Doing It

Melody,

I wish you the best of everything. Hold out for a husband worthy of you.

Love,
Sister Gigle

Guilt-Free Motherhood

How to Raise Great Kids
& Have Fun Doing It

by
Joni Hilton

Covenant Communications, Inc.

Published by Covenant Communications, Inc.
American Fork, Utah

Printed in the United States of America
First Printing: March 1996

01 00 99 98 97 96   10 9 8 7 6 5 4 3 2 1

Library of Congress Cataloging-in-Publication Data

Hilton, Joni, 1956-
    Guilt-Free Motherhood / Joni Hilton.
    p.   cm.
    ISBN 1-55503-898-0
    1. Motherhood—Psychological aspects. 2. Child rearing
3.   Guilt   I. Title
HQ759.H665   1996
306.874'3—dc20   96-1946
                                        CIP

To my husband, Bob, and our children, Richie,
Brandon, Cassidy and Nicole,
all of whom bring me so much joy,
I almost feel guilty.

Contents

Portions of this book have previously appeared in:

Family Circle
McCall's
Parents
Family Fun
Woman's Day
The Los Angeles Times

SECTION ONE

You're a Better Mom Than You Think

CHAPTER 1

Why I Wrote This Book
(And How I Found the Time)

Q: Okay, I have a couple of minutes in the car pool latitudes while I wait for the kids to come pouring out of school. Why'd you write the book?

A: It suddenly hit me that every mom I know feels the weight of a whole van-load of guilt. Work-force moms, stepmoms, stay-at-home moms—nobody's exempt. And today, more than ever, moms stress for success. They're bombarded with expert parenting opinions, kindergarten readiness tests, precocious neighbor kids, and jobs that limit family time. Mothers today are major-league worriers, afraid that their kids won't turn out right . . . and guess who'll be to blame?

Q: Mom, who else?

A: Exactly. "Guiltus Motherus," that species which spans the globe and shows no sign of endangerment. It comes into existence the minute a woman has a baby and realizes, "Uh-oh. I'm *responsible* for this little person!" Before you know it—whammo! Motherhood and Guilt have become synonymous.

Q: So you're saving the mothers of the world with this book.

A: Modesty forbids me to respond (but I can grin).

Q: Where does the guilt come from?

A: Ovaries? Who knows? Actually, I believe any guilt comes from giving less than your best. But with mothering, even truly marvelous moms feel guilty. That kind of guilt gets in the way of good parenting. That's the guilt I want to stamp out.

Q: I thought you just said it's something you automatically acquire when you become a mother.

A: So are stretch marks, but that doesn't mean we have to take it lying down. Guilt pops up when you worry that you're not a good enough mother. But ironically, until we get rid of the guilt, we'll never know how good—and how fun—we can be as mothers. No kid wants a mother with frantic insides. When a mom is serene, confident, buoyantly happy about how she's doing—kids sense it, and feel marvelous about life.

Q: So how does this "guilt guide" do that—how do you start feeling good about your mothering skills?

A: Step by step. In short chapters that they can read between T-ball and piano lessons, moms can learn to do their job guilt-free. Hey. Moms are very ingenious creatures; they can do four loads of laundry, put away the groceries, nurse and diaper a baby, make four peanut butter and jelly sandwiches, coordinate a school fund-raiser, and be the sales manager of a company, all during the same fifteen-minute period. Wiping out guilt should be easier than any of those duties. (And once they do it, they'll know how to avoid such multi-task nightmares.)

Q: It's true that mothers feel tremendous pressure these days. But isn't some of that a good thing?

A: Some chocolate mousse cake is a good thing. I'll explain. Today's intense focus on child-rearing has made all of us a little more thoughtful about how we do it. We weigh decisions more carefully than past generations did. Parents seem more eager to provide all the ingredients that make kids turn out well. That's how the pressure has been a good thing. The problems arise when you go overboard, just like eating that extra slice of mousse cake. And in today's society, we passed overboard some time ago. Some of our sturdiest moms are buckling under.

Q: Those ingredients that make kids turn out well—you have these in the book?

A: Sure; you can't erase guilt without providing them. Knowing you've got your bases covered is one of the big steps in getting rid of guilt. See, lots of moms feel guilty because they don't really know *what* they should be doing. Unfortunately, they assume the worst, and worry that they're leaving out something essential.

Q: So you've found the answer?

A: You're holding it. There really is—finally—a way out from under all the guilt.

Q: What about how you found time to write the book?

A: Oh, that. Well, I do feel just a teensy bit guilty about that part. Hey, c'mon. Nobody's perfect.

·CHAPTER 2

Guilt By Procreation

There you are, seemingly fat as ever despite having just delivered a nine-pound replica of your mother-in-law, and suddenly it's as if some evil giant marched into your room and shoved a huge mirror in front of your face.

"Look at you," the giant sneers. "You're short-tempered, overly sensitive, self-pitying and insecure. How can you possibly raise a *child*? Why, you're no more prepared for this job than to head up a space mission for NASA."

It's true. You tremble. How on earth does anybody keep from making one mistake after another?

"Not only that," the giant continues, "you're undisciplined. You've tried to lose weight— what? Twenty times? Thirty? You're a quitter, and your child is going to copy your poor example."

You gasp. Can it be true? Is your child doomed to inherit your shortcomings?

The giant goes on. "And another thing. You're inept. You have no clue how to feed a baby, and you couldn't diaper a post."

At this point, were it not for your sore stitches, you'd slide right under the covers and out of sight. But you stop. You turn to the giant and say, "Hey—out of my room. Who do you think you are, anyway?"

The giant smiles and shrugs. "I'm your guilt, and you're stuck with me for the rest of your life. Just wait until your baby's a toddler. She's going to burn her feet on your Aunt Evelyn's floor heater and be scarred for life. Your fault, of course. It could be helped. But no, you'd rather go away for the weekend with your husband and leave her in someone else's care.

"On her fifth birthday, you'll forget to bring cupcakes to the kindergarten—after she promised them to all her friends. And the night you decide you're too tired to tell her a bedtime story when she's seven . . . that's the night she'll remember and *never* forgive you for. That, and the cupcakes.

"And then in her teens—"

"STOP!!" You wake up in a sweat, your heart pounding. You feel a certain relief that it was all just a nightmare, but there's still a disquieting specter left behind. Guilt will forever be a monkey on your back; you're sure of it. Unless you can be the perfect mother, you'll destroy your child's chances of happiness. Right?

Dead wrong.

No mother is perfect. I don't care which saint you've plucked off the family tree, or observed among friends, there is no woman in this world who ever mothered perfectly. And you won't either.

But guess what? It's okay. As long as you cover certain basics, you can relax. That doesn't mean it's an easy job, or one you can do without making some sacrifices. But it's a *possible* job—you *can* be a terrific mom. Even if you're not perfect.

As a matter of fact, when a child learns that someone imperfect—Mom—can still be lovable, he realizes the same must be true of him. Imagine the security, joy, and relief of discovering that even if we goof now and then—as we all do—we can still be loved. When we show our children that we can apologize and change, they learn to do the same.

Am I a perfect mother? No way. Am I *striving* to do my best? Yes. And I am not going to let guilt get the upper hand.

Now, certain things go along with parenthood. Things like swaying from side to side even when you *don't* have a baby in your arms, for example. Or double-tying your own shoelaces. Or pointing and saying, "Looky!" to your boss.

And most parents tend to worry, as well. It tugs at our heartstrings when we have to say no to a child's request for a new (but unaffordable) toy. Will our child someday remember this moment as the reason they still resent us? If we don't let them sample every candy bar, will they be "out of it" as kids talk about a certain one in junior high? Will our kids feel deprived because they wore hand-me-downs or had to share a bedroom? Or didn't get sailing lessons? Or couldn't attend a better school? Are we not doing something we can't think of now, but which they are sure to think of later? You could worry yourself into an asylum this way!

During a move, I had to pack one of my kids' bed frames and have him sleep on the floor on a mattress for a few days. I stewed over this prospect for weeks; how could I bed him down on *the floor*? Then, as we were packing, I whispered to him, "This is an Adventure Bed. It's special. If you sleep on *this* one, you'll dream great adventures!"

Well, his brother, who had been listening in, immediately began wailing for his own Adventure Bed, and only after dragging his mattress onto the floor as well, were any of us able to get any sleep. What I had thought would scar them for life turned out to be the grandest gift imaginable!

This reminds me of a girlfriend who has always prepared fabulous meals for her family of eight. She whips up Beef Wellington, scallops, bisques and souffles. Recently two of her kids came home pouting after a visit to their neighbors across the street. "How come you never make good stuff like meat loaf or macaroni and cheese?" they asked.

Sometimes we mistake our own preferences for those of our children. We forget that kids don't feel more loved when we catalog the pantry or sterilize the window sills. We worry that we must give them luxuries and fineries when they'd just as soon eat off paper plates.

We make our children complete chores and work to earn stars, then instead of congratulating ourselves on teaching them responsibility, we look at the undisciplined kids next door and worry that ours will feel unfairly burdened when they compare notes.

We need to step back and get a grip on all this guilt and worry. I wrote an article for a women's magazine once, outlining what I think happens when we try to be perfect parents and compensate 100 per cent for the fact that we're all just human. What you get is one of the worst punishments a child can receive: overparenting.

Overly zealous parents, in an effort to ward off the guilt they probably wouldn't feel if they were covering their bases in the first place, engage in some of the most complicated parenting gymnastics the world has ever seen. I'll show you what I mean.

You're standing in the market, watching an utterly lawless child pour a bag of sugar into the dairy case. Instead of marching the little buzzard right out of the store, the mother purrs, "Use your *words,* Jeffrey. *Tell* me what's bothering you."

Another of these tiptoe parents appears at a library's story time. When the librarian reads the *Three Little Pigs* and comes to the part where the wolf blows down the house and "that was the end of the first little pig," this mother clutches her child to her chest in some kind of maternal choke hold and says, "The pig died, honey. But don't you worry about it. I'm never going to die and leave you, all right?"

Her child stares up and her and typically asks, "And then

what happened?"

All at once it seems the whole world has graduated from Parent College, where text-book children never "act out," where peer pressure is conveniently overlooked, and where moms and dads proudly step up to receive their diplomas for mastering two very bad kinds of parenting, both of which have roots in guilt.

The first is the "never-never-land" theory, to which many moms are charter subscribers. These parents protect their children from pets that might die, games they might lose, pressures they might perceive. In short, from reality.

The second version is the "monster maker" technique, by which parents breathe life into the children's fears simply by zealously calling attention to them, then assuring the kids that such fears are groundless. This process creates a fertile environment for the self-fulfilling prophecy.

Example. Danny's mother picks him up at school and, upon seeing his splashy artwork, says, "Oh, that's very good, Danny. Don't feel bad that you're not drawing people yet. You'll catch up to the others. Don't compare yourself." Small wonder that Danny learns to avoid paints and easels.

Do you see how we got this way? In trying to do the best possible job, we've discovered how much work it is—and how likely we are to flub here and there—so we're overcompensating. We've fretted ourselves into a lather and created a guilt-ridden battleground where we wage war against imaginary obstacles to our child's emotional growth. Hyperanalysis has replaced good old-fashioned love.

How many kids begin worrying about bullies because we have so carefully assured them that we will protect them from the masses of rowdies who will undoubtedly populate future playgrounds? How many toddlers are frightened of monsters at night because we have so thoughtfully explained the impossibility of just such creatures?

And many kids might never even worry about their parents' divorcing if Mommy didn't keep turning to them during "toothpaste cap" quarrels to announce, "Don't worry; Mommy and Daddy are not going to get a divorce."

I'm certainly not against communicating. I'm not against explaining a situation to ease a troubled heart. I'm not against assuring children that their world is happy and secure. I'm not against loving my kids.

But I do object to the kind of guilt that makes us bandage souls that aren't bruised. I'm against stirring up trouble and making monsters where none lived before.

I have four children with active imaginations. If, even jokingly, I said, "Don't worry that I won't pick you up after school," you can guess what they'd think about all day. I might as well tell them not to worry about sharks under their beds.

And it's as if someone has put sharks under *our* beds, too. We worry that we didn't breastfeed. We worry that we breastfed too long. We worry that we didn't toilet train him soon enough. We worry that we toilet trained him too soon. We feel guilty for depriving her, and guilty for spoiling her. We didn't give him enough extra lessons. We gave him too many extra lessons. We weren't home enough. We were home, but we hovered too much.

Enough! It's time to feel secure about the job we're doing as parents. When we can eliminate irrational guilt (and there is a rational kind I'll talk about later), then we can calm our kids' butterflies with nets of normalcy and common sense. Youngsters will then grow up less panicked, less pressured. Their imaginations will be free to roam the worlds of science and literature without fretting that a meteor might crush their house, or that what happened to Bambi might happen to them.

And if we tear up our tickets to never-never-land, we'll be able to teach our children not only how to cope with life's disappointments, but how to make such setbacks work in their favor.

When my eldest son was three, I saw what can happen when we stop trying to make every experience palatable to our offspring. Richie had been in the kitchen with me, pretending to fish with a strip of plastic for a fishing pole. He caught it under the refrigerator and it snapped in half.

Heartbroken, Richie seized the two pieces and looked at me with the desperate expression of a child who thinks his parents can fix anything. "It's broken," he wailed. "Can you fix it?"

I shook my head, almost as sad as he. "I'm sorry, honey. That can't be fixed."

His chin quivered as he stared at the hopeless condition of his toy. Then, just as I was about to launch into my overkill speech about how it didn't have to spoil the day and how life was still worth living and how sometimes terrible things happen to wonderful people, Richie chirped, "Hey! Now I have *two* fishing poles!"

Darned if he didn't. Kids also have a lot of the answers to life's various surprises—if only we remain silent long enough to let them surface.

So send out the Guilt Giant and stand back occasionally. Enjoy being a mother who knows the difference between parenting and overparenting. It's one of the first steps to guilt-free mothering. Your kids will thank you for it.

SECTION TWO

Ten Traits Every
Child Needs

CHAPTER 3

The Spoon In The Road

Most victims of Guiltus Motherus will turn right to this section to see a checklist, holding their breath and crossing their fingers. *Am I measuring up? Am I giving my child every possible trait, or turning him into a chain-saw murderer by leaving one out?* Stop worrying so much!

On the other end of the spectrum we have the completely irresponsible mom. Subscribing to the Roseanne Barr school of motherhood, these moms might echo that comedienne's line, "If my husband gets home and the kids are still alive, I figure I've done my job."

Somewhere between the two, and hopefully erring on the side of Mother Number One, is a mom who is doing her best to provide growth opportunities for her children. She doesn't completely take over and force-feed the traits into their bloodstream (which doesn't work, anyway); she simply does like you and I do. She reads such a list, then strives to guide her youngsters into opportunities where they learn by themselves. Independently, they'll develop characteristics which will give them pretty good odds on being happy and emotionally successful adults one day. We can't *make* our children succeed. But we can give them some tools and encouragement.

Also, our own feelings of guilt are greatly diminished when we see that we actually are providing the basics. If we're not, we can start now to give our children these kinds of experiences. Don't panic or start feeling overwhelmed; this book is to *reduce* guilt, not *induce* it. When you read the following list and discover (as we all would) that you fall short somewhere, don't despair. Before you're through with this book, you'll learn how to plug any holes and feel great about your ability to mother.

Remember, one of the ways to reduce guilt is by checking yourself against a realistic standard (emphasize *realistic* here) and seeing that, all in all, you're doing fine.

Keep in mind the words of Dr. Jack Shonkoff of the University of Massachusetts Medical School, who was quoted in *Parenting Magazine* as saying that "Very good parents who raise very good children are going to make half a dozen child-rearing mistakes a day."

CHOICES. Every child needs some free agency. It seems a crime against the soul of man to rob a person of his preferences, but we see it all the time. Too many parents do all the thinking and choosing for their kids until the children are big, lumbering high school sophomores who can't decide whether or not to sharpen a pencil without Mom's opinion.

Obviously, you can't let a four-year-old decide to play with matches or give him the keys to the car. But she can certainly choose which shirt to wear, or which kind of fruit to have with lunch. My second son, Brandon, is a great one for independent choices. His pre-school teachers were always amused by the Superman capes, firefighter hats, and various other garments that he would wear to school. Sometimes a shirt would be intentionally inside out, or he'd wear mismatching shoes. But always, there was a personal statement in it.

This same child casually announced one day that his name was now "Spike." My husband and I exchanged frozen glances, then decided to go along with it. What better way to reaffirm our delight in his individuality? I thought about the name Spike. It has spunk; it's the name of a kid with style to spare and a great sense of humor. Somebody named Spike is going to be surrounded by admirers, leading the pack with confidence and flair. It's a name that pretty well describes Brandon, as a matter of fact. When we told the story to a friend of ours one evening, the fellow scratched his chin, turned to his wife and said, "Hey, you know? I think maybe I'll change *my* name to Spike."

One time I was talking to my boys about tough decisions. I said that one method is to write down all the options on a piece of paper. Sometimes you can divide it into two columns of pros and cons, I said. Soon my eldest, Richie, said, "How come they call it a fork in the road when a fork has four points and the road always has two? They should call it a Y in the road."

I agreed. But then I explained that with most decisions, there are often several choices. In the Y road, for example, two more choices are to sit down or go back. The next-oldest, Brandon, finally decided that the proper phrase should be a *spoon* in the road, because on a surface that wide, you could choose almost anything.

Giving kids freedom of choice when we can, builds tremendous self-esteem. When kids learn that they are actually capable of making decisions, they feel a swelling of confidence and a delight in their own judgment—even when they fail.

EVEN WHEN THEY FAIL? Sure; they discover solutions, they learn what not to do next time, they learn that their family will still love them when they goof, and they discover the law of consequences. Children whose parents have spared them any failure are at a tremendous disadvantage in life. In fact, as you look back, didn't your mistakes teach you more than your successes?

Case in point. I grew up near a ski resort and took skiing lessons all winter as a little girl. I didn't know it was a phobia at the time, but I was acutely afraid of heights. My heart would pound and my stomach would tie in knots the entire time I rode the ski lift. I had no clue that I was any different than the others, who, I simply figured, must be braver souls than I. And then, to make matters worse, I was a klutz. For six years I endured this, trying to learn to ski and get past my fear of falling from the ski lift. Some parents would have pulled their child out of the sport in the face of such slow progress. Anyone could see that the other children were becoming expert skiers, while I struggled hopelessly behind.

This is the kind of story that ends with my telling you about my gold medal in the downhill competition, right? Afraid not. Today I'm still just an intermediate skier, so I suppose you could say I failed. Or did I? My fear of heights is conquered. I look back with great pride that I slew my phobia dragon, and *equal* pride that I persevered at a sport for which I didn't have any natural talent. And, I can ski, by George. I may not look like an Olympic contender, but I feel confident on almost any hill. "Not winning" somehow feels like winning, anyway, because I *chose* to keep skiing when others might have quit. Today I'll tackle just about anything, and I expect to succeed.

Sometimes the kids for whom everything comes easily never learn those stick-to-it skills they'll need later when they finally do have a challenge. Over and over I've watched children (usually the second-borns) struggle in the shadow of a highly achieving sibling. Then, in their teens or just after, something happens. The one who sailed along effortlessly is now out in the real world, encountering gale storms without a sail or rudder. And the struggler, who developed muscle in the school of hard knocks, picked up a survival skill or two that helps him navigate well and even enjoy the ride! Suddenly the "less talented" sibling edges out in front. Letting our kids struggle through their decisions helps them build strength they'll need later.

Often the decisions our children have to make are moral ones. Again, we must resist intervening. Once you teach your children correct principles, you're really obligated to put that knowledge to the test and let them try their wings. The whole point in parenting is to raise *independent*, capable adults, right? So how can they learn independence without getting a little practice at it?

One father in a very religious family comes to mind. He'd done a great job raising several children, and felt he had taught them how to make wise decisions. His teenage son, whom he had raised to go to church on Sundays, came to him one Saturday and explained that his friends had invited him to go waterskiing the following morning, instead of attending church.

The father was reading the paper, and turned the page. "Well? What did you decide?" the father asked.

The son gulped. "I thought . . . I was asking you if you think it would be okay if I go."

The father refused to grant or deny permission. He simply smiled. "Son," he said, "I've already taught you all you need to know to make that decision. I've done my part, and I can answer to God quite happily about the job I've done. If you decide to go waterskiing, that will be your own free choice. You'll be the one to answer for it, not me."

The son just stared at his clear-conscience father, who happily continued to read the paper, entirely absolved of guilt. The weight of the responsibility, which had now shifted to the boy as an "adult," truly stunned him. Suddenly he wasn't a little kid wheedling to get out of a duty, or trying to talk Dad into something. He was someone his dad respected, whom he trusted to choose wisely.

The standards you select in your own family may or may not include Sabbath activities. But you'll still want your children to adhere to the ethics and values you've taught them, and to make decisions independently, accepting full credit or blame for their choices.

It takes great strength to hold back, to resist the pull we feel to jump in and direct our kids' lives. It's so much easier to make their bed than to watch as they take fifteen minutes and then still don't do it right. But it's a wise parent who gives her children space, and freedom to make decisions on their own. You want to reduce guilt? Give your child choices. And by the way, the teenager went to church.

CHAPTER 4

This Corner of My Heart

Second on the list is *ADMIRATION*. Rather than a trait, this one is a gift, a feeling your child can cherish in his heart. The knowledge that your parents really and truly *admire* you gives a level of security unsurpassed by any accolade the world can bestow. Not only that, but admiration isn't really tied to performance or accomplishments. It's tied to character. When you deeply admire someone, you have to know their personality with faults and strengths combined. Convince your child that you love her completely, regardless of anything she may ever do to disappoint you. You may not approve of all her choices down the road, but you will always admire her inner self. You will look to her for opinions, you will enjoy hearing her outlooks and sharing her humor, and you will always, always want to pick her brain for feelings and ideas. You see that child as a well from which you love to drink.

My father, a university professor, used to ask me to review speeches and papers he would write. Not so unusual, you may think to yourself. After all, I'm a writer, right? But Dad was asking my opinion when I was *eight years old*! It didn't strike me as unusual at the time; I was too young to know that most adults don't ask children for critiques. But it convinced me that Dad valued my opinion. I took his requests seriously, and gave him the most thoughtful answers I could. He always listened carefully to my feedback, just as if I were an associate of equal training.

This doesn't mean we become artificial. To this day I think Dad wanted my input, simply because he deeply believed that kids see a lot of things adults miss.

My favorite photo of my father is a candid shot. The picture is actually of me talking and laughing with some friends. But the photographer happened to catch my father in the background, and there on his face is the perfect expression of admiration, as he gazes at his daughter with pure love, unaware that anyone can see him.

We need to convey to our children that we truly adore them and think they're pretty terrific—that even if we weren't related, we'd still want them for a buddy. This kind of love transcends the "love of duty" many children suspect their parents feel. It ascends into delight and real admiration. And it doesn't mean we overpraise; just let your child know that there is a special corner of your heart that fits only her, exactly and perfectly.

Be more than a parent who spews out directives. Genuinely like your child, and let him know often. This foundation of affection can pave the rocky paths of adolescence, too. Parents who share hobbies, humor, and friendship with their children find their relationships in pretty good repair after their kids navigate the difficult teen years.

Admiration and praise are magnetic to all of us. We find ourselves attracted to friends who really enjoy us. If we aren't conveying that kind of glad-to-see-you attitude in our home, it won't take long for our children to find it elsewhere.

Shortly after my father's death, I ran across a girlfriend's exhusband. In a made-for-movie sequence of events, "Joe" had taken drugs, become a punk-rocker, and their marriage had dissolved. When I mentioned that my father had died, Joe immediately shared a most telling story about Dad. At a party at my home once, he and Dad had gotten to talking about music. Dad was an opera buff and classical music lover, yet never closed-minded. Joe was so impressed that my father had said, "You know, I've been listening to some of that punk music, and I think some of it has certain merits. I can see some musical innovation in a few of the songs."

For the first time—maybe in too long—Joe had felt accepted. No—*admired*. Somebody had finally said something positive, and it made him feel important. That feeling belongs in the heart of every one of us—and in the heart of every child.

Instead of gasping, "Oh, kill me now, my son's pierced his ear, life's over—" why don't we give him a bit of credit and say, "Gee . . . wouldn't old Mr. Grickson look better if he pierced his ear, too?" So it isn't a choice *you* would have made. It's done. And your son undoubtedly knows your preferences. He's simply hoping you'll tolerate his, as he tolerates yours.

It's a little like letting your child call himself Spike. It's saying to him, "You know, if someone as clever as you thought of that, it must be a pretty good idea." Kids who hear these kinds of messages start thinking of themselves as good people. And when they believe in their own worth and value, their actions will mirror their inner beliefs.

CHAPTER 5

You Did It!

Third is the gift of *ACHIEVEMENT*. Not every child is blessed with a perfect pitching arm, or perfect pitch. Yet every child needs to feel an inner sense of pride in accomplishment. Kids who aren't given the chance to excel never get to savor their achievements. Without learning to work hard and then to enjoy and relish one's work, you're asking for a pretty unhappy adulthood. Few of us can coast through life without doing some work; yet if we never learn the satisfaction that comes from mastering something, we sentence ourselves to frustration.

And it's more than learning how to work. It isn't just tacking up a list of chores, and making sure your kid does each one. It's learning *competence*. I still remember the surge of self esteem I felt when, as a little girl, I cooked an entire dinner for the family. None of my friends had done that yet, but I asked for the chance and my parents let me give it a try. I proved myself capable, and it felt like taking a giant step toward adulthood.

You hear it among kids all the time. They brag about what level of Nintendo they're on, what skateboard tricks they can do, which reader they're in at school. The desire to excel at something is within each of us, and usually spans many subjects. Some parents let their children take music lessons, play on a team, or pursue some other interest that brings satisfaction. Giving children the chance to discover their strengths will stay with them throughout life, and give them the self-confidence to know that they can learn anything they set their minds to.

Setting a goal and struggling toward it teaches another important lesson we have to learn in life: to delay gratification. Kids are fun-seekers, and that's a wonderful element of life (for grownups, too). I'm not suggesting we take that away. But it seems we try to make *everything* fun. And it just plain isn't. The story is told that someone once said to the pianist Paderewski, "I'd give my life to play like that." To which Paderewski replied, "I did."

Success and accomplishment require persistence and sacrifice. If we train our kids to think that every task has to be a game or a pleasure, we rob them of learning how to persevere through the pain. And isn't that essential? Look at your marriage! Look at your career! Can someone who quits when the going gets tough possibly succeed?

This doesn't mean we strip our children of all silly giggling or the occasional lazy afternoons. We all need to rejuvenate ourselves with interludes of relaxation. But children need to see these breaks as just what they are: needed rests in an otherwise productive life. Look at life as if it were a piece of music: highs and lows, loud notes and soft ones, fast notes and slow notes, and certainly some rests. If the music has no rests, it will be a frantic, tedious piece. But if you have *only* rests, there's no music at all!

Our second son, Brandon, is a marvel. He is absolutely fascinated by anything medieval, and loves fantasies about knights and dragons. After trying every sport imaginable and waiting for one to "take," we finally hit upon fencing. Magic! The kid is hooked. When we left Los Angeles for a smaller city in the midwest where there was no fencing instruction for youth, I drove him each week to another town, to take part in a college fencing club.

His other love turned out to be chess, but our new city had no chess club for children. I combed the town for a local chess expert to instruct, and started an after-school chess club at my son's elementary school. Forty children showed up! Brandon may or may not pursue fencing and chess as he grows older. But I am giving him every chance to excel at the things he enjoys trying.

Like Brandon, many children's interests will be out of the ordinary. Or a child might develop as simple a talent as setting the table well. It might be the ability to comfort another child. It could be an obedient heart, or strong faith. It could be a wonderful sense of humor, or a positive outlook.

Ask yourself, What am I doing to help my child gain a sense of accomplishment? Am I exposing her to varied interests so she can find a hobby or activity that excites her? Do I provide library books, lessons, excursions and activities when I can? (And this does not need to be an overwhelming load; letting kids get bored and think for themselves is a sadly neglected activity these days!) Do I give encouragement when my child tries something new? Am I teaching my child to discipline herself and helping her set goals, then work toward them? Chances are, you're right on track.

I know an extremely capable woman in her sixties, Doris, who has marvelous self- esteem. She traces it to a simple thing her mother did when she was a child. As family or neighborhood needs arose, her mother would say, "Oh, Doris can do that." Initially she would think, "I *can?*" But, she reasoned, if her mother thought she could do it, it must be true. And so she tried, expecting to succeed, and found that her mother was right.

One more word about achievement: It can be overdone. While every child needs a feeling of competence—or better yet, excellence—we can err on the side of pushing too hard, and leave kids frustrated as they fall short of Mom's goals. Along with high expectations for our children, we need to make certain we give them approval and love *just because they're ours*, not only because they've achieved a goal.

I recommend three ways to do this. First, take occasional strolls through the family photo album. Don't hide your delight in your child as a baby. Lay it on thick. Wasn't he darling? Wasn't he covered with kisses? Wasn't he the apple of everyone's eye? An older child may squirm at this, but underneath he is learning an important concept. Point out that he was positively adored even before he had garnered a single accomplishment. Love is not tied to accomplishments. It is simply there, no matter what he does.

Second, don't save all your rewards for completed tasks. Give your kids special treats "just because." Not every excursion, ice cream cone, or gift has to be tied to a goal sheet. In fact, employers find that occasional bonuses "just because" yield greater productivity than reserving extras solely for when goals are met. It makes us feel appreciated and renews our motivation. And in a family setting, it helps our kids realize that our love is not tied to their actions, but to them *personally*.

The third way to keep kids from feeling rushed to excel, is to allow for slip-ups without overreacting. If your child is basically a good student, and getting back one bad test score is not a major trend, then don't give a major reaction. Likewise, if he's a good ballplayer and he has one bad game, shrug it off like the *game* that it is. (Besides, if you don't, he'll wonder if you really believe in his skills, or if you think one stumble could really throw him off permanently!)

Project the idea that your family stands for doing one's best and enjoying the rewards of discipline, but don't create a climate of rigid inflexibility. That leads to perfectionism and diminishes, rather than builds, self-esteem.

CHAPTER 6

Time Out For Time

TIME is the rarest commodity these days, but the most valuable one. No matter what you're doing, when you know you should be with your kids instead, you'll feel guilty. And all the guilt books in the world won't build a big enough bridge to cover that chasm. (That's the "appropriate" guilt I mentioned earlier—Guilt for Good Reason—and I'll come back to it in the next section).

If swelling to the size of an adult hippo for nine months didn't tip you off that parenting was going to involve some sacrifice, let me reiterate: Parenting is going to involve some sacrifice. Of course, it also involves immense happiness and joy. But it can't be done properly without investing sheer *time*. Period.

A religious leader, M. Russell Ballard, said that to see our children grow, succeed, and take their place in society and in the Lord's kingdom is an eternal reward worth *any* amount of inconvenience or sacrifice. Did you think it would be *easy* to raise a well-adjusted adult? Did you think you could shrug guilt off without *some* effort? Of course not. And even if you subtract the spiritual elements of that quote, you know that the sacrifices you make for your child will indeed bring rewards.

We hear so often about quality time. Funny thing is, we only hear about it from grownups. Kids don't seem to differentiate between *quality* time and *quantity* time. They simply want to *be* with you. I picture a weary Mom and Dad coming through the door from work while their son, perched in front of a computer game, scarcely looks up. Mom and Dad try to invent a quality conversation (after all, bedtime for Billy is in one hour, and there's no time to spare), but Billy seems uninterested. Oh, well, deduce his wise parents, Billy is an independent spirit who simply doesn't require much attention from them.

What would happen to a marriage treated that way? Your husband drags through the front door, grabs the phone from your hand, pulls you away from the radio contest where you were about to win five thousand dollars, and pulls you into the bedroom for some now-or-never, weary intimacy. I know, I know, there are a few wives who would welcome such behavior.

But if it didn't seem like he genuinely cared about you, if it seemed like he'd read an article about spending X amount of time with you because he's *supposed* to . . . you know as well as I where that marriage would be heading: straight to the rocks.

Kids deserve better than our daily leftovers, too. They deserve to have us reachable when *they* want to be with us, not just when we will consent to be with them. Maybe thirty minutes earlier, Billy did indeed want to talk. But not now. We're the same way, aren't we? Time . . . and timing. It makes all the difference.

When you've promised to spend time with your child, don't let *anything* intrude upon it. Let your kids know that they come first, and a date to get a hamburger with Jeremy is a lot more important than someone from the office stopping by.

I know a girl whose mother canceled a meeting so she

could listen to her daughter's anguish over a heartbreak, and dry the daughter's tears herself. The girl may forget the boy who made her cry, but she will always remember that when she really needed her, Mom was there and put her daughter first.

Most mothers today work outside the home. There are times when you have to leave your children in order to put bread on the table. To keep from feeling guilty, let your children know that despite the necessity of being gone sometimes, your *favorite* time is time spent with them. "I'd rather be with you than do anything else," is a vital message for every child.

If you can possibly adjust your schedule, or defer your career until your children are older, you will never regret the decision. I take that back. All kids go through monstrous moments. Let's face it, there are days! But overall, you will know in your heart that you're doing right by the people you brought into the world. Would you buy a house plant that needed watering every half hour, and then take on a full-time job away from home? Take a hard look at the commitment you made when you decided to become a parent. Can you do this job (and it's the toughest job on the planet) part-time?

I know; we don't all have a choice. But *if* you have a choice, make it carefully.

I'm going to make a prediction. I think we'll see an odd phenomenon in our society in a few years. We'll see some terrific kids raised by two parents who truly care, whose dads weren't afraid to apologize or express love, and who are beautifully adjusted.

But we'll also see the results of neglect in frightening numbers. Affluent kids who were raised by nannies, while their career-driven parents did their own thing, will suddenly have much in common with their poverty-stricken counterparts who had no visible father, and whose exhausted mothers had no choice but to work three jobs just to survive. Both neglected groups will be selfish, angry, greedy, and unable to sustain relationships. You and I, as taxpayers, will pay a high price for their inadequate self-esteem and their undisciplined behavior.

But whether full-time parenting is an option for you or not, you need to make your choice and then project enjoyment of that decision. Studies have shown that the children of both stay-at-home and work-away mothers do best when they know their moms are happy and fulfilled.

Both kinds of mothers can arrange to spend one-on-one time with their children, to really make memories and grow close. If you have several children, this takes some creativity, but it's essential to give each child a moment in the sun, a certainty that they are individually special.

A friend of mine, raised on a cattle farm, remembers that every time her father had to go into town, one of the eight children would get to ride along in the pickup truck. She remembers those times alone with her father as wonderful moments when they could truly share feelings and grow close.

Some of my most cherished childhood memories are of times alone with either of my parents. I recall matinee-and-ice cream dates with my dad, hiking or fishing with him, and making cookies with my mother. I looked forward to these dates the way I anticipated Christmas. Not only did we have fun times, but the symbolism was monumental: I *mattered*; I really did. My parents wanted to set aside time with *just me*! It was a self-esteem high. Even a mom who finds she must be absent from the home for forty hours a week, can still arrange for those magical moments alone with each child.

Today Bob and I carry on this tradition, and set aside "date days" for each of our four children. It takes some sacrifice and schedule juggling, but the dividends are worth it. Not only do we sense a closer bond with each child, but our reactions to that child *the rest of the time* are calmer, more understanding, more loving.

Sometimes there are snatches of time as we take a child to a lesson or an appointment. We invite a child to help us prepare dinner, or to come along on an errand. Don't discount these daily experiences, simply because you are doubling up to accomplish something else. It's still a moment of shared intimacy. Long drives without distraction have sometimes provided moments when my children have opened up the most, and shared their deepest feelings. I took my five-year-old son with me to a recent appointment, and the woman I met with said, "You take your children with you everywhere you can, don't you?" I smiled and nodded. Mom's my job.

One way to have some daily togetherness is to squeeze in just five minutes to share a project or an activity. You might be thinking, "Five minutes? You can't do *anything* in five minutes." But you'd be surprised. Every morning we take five minutes to play together. We set aside our car keys, homework, backpacks, etc., and take part in a stimulating experiment, a goofy game, a dazzling discovery. This jump-starts our kids' minds, and it makes mornings less frenzied, more organized. Everyone gets a move on, because they don't want to miss Project Time.

I wrote a book about this for Running Press publishers. It's called *Five Minute Miracles: 373 Quick Daily Projects for You and Your Kids to Share*. It's filled with hundreds of things you can do in five minutes, just using what you already have around the house. But you can design your own projects, too. You could find your five-minute slot in the evenings, at bedtime, or whenever it works for you.

Be flexible and willing to "seize the moment." Cancel whatever you must to take advantage of that one day of perfect kite-flying weather. Break the routine and live a life where you dictate the time, rather than having time dictate to you. Goethe said, "Things which matter most must never be at the mercy of things which matter least."

A friend of mine with nine children takes ten minutes with each child as she puts them to bed at night, hearing something about their day and giving each of them a sincere compliment. Beyond the time she has already spent with them, they look forward to their "goodnight time" with her. (And how would *you* like 365 compliments a year?) Yes, it takes her an hour and a half. It's her favorite hour and a half of the day.

Bob and I find bedtime especially sweet, also. Our ritual includes reading, prayers, and lying down briefly with each child—sometimes to sing, whisper silly stories, tickle, snuggle, or stroke their heads into slumber. It's a small investment with a gigantic yield: a strong base— an unbreakable one, we hope—of closeness and friendship with our children.

Some families make weekly time for each child. I know one mother who has a mother-daughter date every week with her ten-year-old girl. Thursday nights are theirs alone to go to dinner and talk about whatever they wish. Sometimes they attend plays, go shopping, or indulge in a new hairstyle. The rest of the week may be a chaotic jumble of dashing to work, meetings, school and sports, but Thursday night is . . . ahhh. . . .

A father of six has another way to spend one-on-one time each week. He calls it The Personal Interview. He meets privately with each child on Sundays to ask them about their week. Are they getting along with their siblings? Is everything all right at school? How are they feeling inside? Are they happy with their friends? What's unfair? What's wonderful? It's not a stressful interview, but rather a friendly chat—a chance to let off steam, to voice opinions, to hug and express love to one another. Each child looks forward to his appointed time of day for his "date" with Dad. This may not sound spontaneous, but spontaneity can be overrated. If we're always waiting for a natural moment of open communication, sometimes it never comes.

Depending on your schedule and the number of your children, a monthly date might be a good fit. Bob and I find this works well if we want to give several hours to each child, and build real date-like memories. The one rule we have is that once a date is made, it cannot be cancelled or postponed. It's one of those kooky laws, that the minute you make a date with your kid, five phone calls will come through requesting that same slice of time. So Bob and I have decided ahead of time that we will not be budged. We want to send the distinct message to our children that nothing else matters more than they do. (Picture your mate agreeing to a date with you, then worming out of it every time in favor of work or other offers.) And ask yourself: What would you say if this were your child's wedding? Nothing could make you miss it. Happily, we've discovered that instead of offending bosses, friends, and others who need us, they come away impressed that we're so devoted to our family.

Occasionally we choose an activity and take our children to a surprise we've planned. An outing that might be too expensive for all to enjoy—great theater or opera tickets, for example—might fit a budget perfectly if it's only the two of you.

You might design a treasure hunt, learn a new sport, see a free exhibit, pitch in to help the community, share a hobby, make something together, tour a local factory or museum, explore a nearby town, or just lean back and watch the clouds.

But most of the time, we let the children design the dates. Sometimes they choose things I love—a nature walk in the woods, shopping for antiques, a new restaurant, or gathering shells at the beach. More often, they choose things they like (and would you want it any other way?).

As the mother of athletic children (who has remarkably hidden the fact that she detests nearly every sport), I have spent afternoons throwing and chasing baseballs (why do they have to be so hard?), swinging at and chasing tennis balls (who designed such large courts?), and hurling bowling balls toward pins unknown, then feeling my kids pat me on the shoulder as my balls bounce into the gutters.

I have stared at slot cars zooming around and around and around the same track, until my eyes couldn't focus properly. I have buckled in and driven little race cars around and around yet another track until my arms couldn't steer properly.

I have watched with the boredom that approaches hysterical screaming as my eldest son has tried to beat every game in a noisy video arcade.

I have kept from drumming my fingers impatiently as one son combed through an army/navy surplus store until he found and bought a detonated hand grenade.

I have been dragged to the butcher shop in a seedy part of town, to see whole pig heads and lamb heads in the meat case, and then quietly programmed my brain not to have nightmares about it.

So why do I put myself through this? Because sometime during the date, my kid looks up at me and gives me this broad, shining grin that comes straight up from his toes. It's not the "Bye, Mom!" quick kiss and smile as they dash away. It's not the "Oh, hi," smile when they come home from school. It's the pure filet of childhood joy—it's a kid living the kind of life you always hoped he would. And I was there to see it.

CHAPTER 7

A Friend Indeed!

Is it possible to give our children the *ABILITY TO SELECT FRIENDS*? We can make a big difference. Every kid needs to like himself enough that he won't stand for people to abuse or neglect him. He'll insist on decent treatment from respectful friends. Parents can genuinely help their kids analyze why they hang around with the kids they do. By asking questions early on, and being available with ideas about how to handle social problems that arise on the playground, parents can lay important groundwork in teaching kids how to pick good friends later.

The power of peer pressure is astounding. Ask any parent of teenagers. If your children learn to choose happy achievers for friends, the pressure will be to excel and succeed. If you notice your child being the victim of a bully, or being the bully herself, it's time to talk. What areas of life are feeling out of control to her? Where is she unhappy? What would she like to change? Help your child take one step at a time toward being socially confident and secure.

We also need to teach our kids how to *be* good friends. Don't shrug and ignore it when your kid bursts out with some rude remark to a friend. Take him aside later, and explain how he's coming across. If you see selfishness, bossiness, timidity—

anything that's an obstacle—help your child see it, too, and help him come up with solutions.

Through example and discussion, you can teach your children consideration of others' feelings, keeping trusts, being loving—all the qualities that make a good friend.

A young woman recalled that her mother sent her to her room for having a sassy attitude one morning before school. Worried that she'd miss the bus and angry at her mother, the girl fired off another retort. Her mother followed her into the bedroom and said, "Obviously, I'm not going to win the Miss Congeniality award today." The girl stifled a laugh, then her mother said, "But maybe *you* will." This mother was clearly willing to sacrifice her own popularity to teach her daughter how to have friends and get along with others.

Sometimes our children latch onto friends in an abnormally dependent way. This is a time to have a long talk about what that person is providing that your child herself is not. What need is that person meeting? Is there a deficiency in your child's personality which this other child possesses? Why doesn't your child feel content without that person? It is essential that children overcome this problem, or they also will choose a marriage partner for the wrong reasons. Often a child will choose someone more popular, funny, or with more "personality," to make up for areas where they feel they are lacking. We need to help our children feel better about themselves—and whole—so that they don't "need" a surrogate personality figure to fill in the blanks.

And some children pick weaklings so that they can dominate. Again, these habits will stay throughout life (and ruin marriages, jobs, etc.) if not worked out while kids are young.

The best friendships are those where power is shared. The two people may be vastly different in other ways, but no one is the submissive doormat, or the complete ruler.

Some young people—and some adults, too—kid themselves

by thinking that others don't influence them. They make comments such as, "I'm still the same person, no matter who I'm with." Ha! None of us are. We are all influenced by the people we're with. Anybody who tells you they act the exact same way around every person in their world, isn't being honest with you or with himself! The first step is to admit that we are all malleable, we are all affected by the friends we choose. Don't your children act differently around their peers than they act around your great Aunt Ethel, who never liked them? And don't *you*?

I tell my children to surround themselves with people who bring out their best. If someone makes you feel snobby, greedy, sneaky, defensive, selfish, guilty—or a hundred other negative things—then realize that this person *is* influencing you, and get away from them! I tell them to pick people who accept you as you are, so you don't have to be false around them. Pick people who make you strive to be your best, people who are fun to be around, who brighten up the world, who stimulate new thoughts.

The same advice works for *us*! Don't we have friends who bring us down and make us feel bad every time we talk to them? I once had a foul-weather girlfriend who was exactly like this. Whenever my life was in a slump, or a roller-coaster dip, she was there to commiserate. I mistook her gladness in my misfortune for sympathy and caring. It was as if she was feeding off my unhappiness, eager to give me advice (though the advice was never very encouraging). But when things would turn around and my roller coaster was riding high again, she would suddenly change. Our conversations became peppered with comments about my being too busy for her. She would remark that she certainly wouldn't envy my successes, because they were much too taxing. Was she jealous? I only knew that I dreaded sharing any joys with her, because she was there with a pin waiting to pop my balloon, draining me of all enthusiasm.

When I finally realized the stress this relationship was having on my life, I cooled it. Sometimes we need to repair our own friendships (or lop off the damaging ones) so our children will see from our example how to feel enough self-esteem that they won't settle for a friend who doesn't have their best interests at heart.

Change is tough for all of us, but sometimes we need to take drastic steps to help our children into better friendships. First, we must teach our children to choose wisely from the pool of candidates. You can move to different schools, even move to another state; but if your child hasn't conquered her need to identify with a rough crowd, for example, she'll only find another.

If your child *wants* good friends, and is simply a victim of unfortunate circumstances, you need to get her into a better situation. Sometimes a child becomes the target of cruelty at a certain school, sometimes an entire neighborhood is devoid of playmates (or good ones, anyway), and sometimes a child simply needs a wider selection.

Take the trouble to enroll your child in some extra classes for the social benefit of it. Let her meet peers who share her interests. Talk with her teacher and arrange play dates with kids she particularly likes, even if they aren't geographically close. Let her meet and form relationships with others outside her usual circle.

What if it's a quantity issue? If the problem is that your child doesn't have enough friends, but if *you* are the only one worried about it, back off. Lots of kids are perfectly content alone. By forcing her to spend time with people she doesn't enjoy, you only make her miserable. If she can play contentedly by herself, hurray! This is a sign of maturity. Just make sure she's happy that way, then leave it alone. We shouldn't remake our children into clones of ourselves. Children need to decide how many friends are enough.

CHAPTER 8

I Know Who I am

Kids need *A SENSE OF SELF*, a feeling of belonging. They need answers to the important questions: Who am I? What kind of family are we? Call it heritage or tradition—it's what tells a child who he is and what's expected of him. A friend of mine whose ancestors include some of our nation's founders has said to her children, "What this means is that you must contribute." Her family identity is one of civic pride and patriotism.

Some people search their family tree and draw up a chart to evoke pride in forebears. Others make a bright family flag that depicts their values, or they might create a family song or cheer. Family reunions elicit feelings of pride in heritage, and make even the littlest child feel he's an important part of the clan.

Define for your child what it means to be a (your last name here). Many times I've said to my children, "In our family we keep our word." Or, "We have integrity in our family. We do the right thing." It gives them a standard to live up to, an inner confidence that, simply because they belong, they come from what used to be called "good stock."

I believe in hanging family photographs on the wall. It helps children define themselves as happy kids when they see pictures of themselves laughing with their family. We also prominently display artwork and certificates that mark their achievements. Some families have monthly awards for good deeds, or a "You Are Special" plate to honor outstanding events.

Family traditions, vacations, and holidays all create a definition of who we are and what we do. For some families, this includes a religion, or at least a set of moral codes. If not a religion, children should be taught a value system that encourages love of others and a striving to do one's best.

One family I know made a Family Constitution that everyone contributed to. It beautifully set forth their beliefs, dreams, and loyalty to one another.

Another idea I like is to create a family flag. Let the children choose the symbols and colors, even the motto. Some good mottos I've heard used are "Return with Honor," "Love, Service & Unity," "Together Forever," "Heaven on Earth," "United We Stand," and even the great old Musketeer slogan, "One For All and All For One."

A family flag can unify a family reunion, and can be reproduced on stationery and T-shirts if you like. Add streamers with each child's name printed on it—or a streamer every year, listing another virtue you espouse. Some families even make up a family cheer. All these things promote a feeling of belonging.

Of course, the best way to give children standards and ideals is to live them yourself. Example truly is the best teacher. But when you write them up, or display an ancestor's photo or a family flag, you somehow make it more official.

Some time ago, Bob and I were doing some genealogy, filling in the blanks between Bob and a well-known ancestor, General Thomas Sumter. Sumter was a revolutionary war hero, a senator, a swashbuckler, a guerilla warfare expert, and a feisty fighter who was said to enjoy the blood of the battle as much as the victory. He was a bigger-than-life hero kind of guy, who turned over a canoe and brought in six renegades. And he's the one Fort Sumter in South Carolina was named for. Needless to say, it is pure fun to research such a colorful relative, and to note the similarities between him and Bob, who's the same sort of daredevil as his great-great-great.

But what most surprised me was when I came across a painting of General Sumter, and gasped at the similarity in their faces—Bob's mother more so, and his grandfather even more so. "I'll bet the ol' general gave his wife gray hair, too," I muttered. Bob smirked and I flipped the page. Then I secretly went about hiring an artist to duplicate the oil painting at nearly life-size.

Needless to say, it's one of the first things we'd grab if we had a fire. Every day we pass this painting, and we talk about Sumter's qualities (his *good* qualities) to our children, reminding them of their heritage.

Some time ago, my uncle was tracing some family history on my side, and couldn't track down the father of a certain boy. Time and again, the leads all stopped in England, where there had never been a house, and where now stands a hospital. After researching a bit more, my uncle discovered that this was indeed where the boy was born, but that his mother was proprietor of, shall we say, a house of ill repute.

"Well," I scoffed to Bob that night, "I guess I can hang my madame next to your general, and we'll have a perfectly balanced ancestry!"

Okay, so the madame never made it into portraiture. (And you thought *you* had a lot to feel guilty about!) But we've found plenty of other relatives to honor and emulate. By doing so, we give our kids a definition of their worth, a solid picture of who they are and where they fit in this world.

CHAPTER 9

The Safety Net

Kids need to know that if they need help, we're there for them. They need to know that, though we wish only the best for them, we'll still love them through the worst. If they make mistakes or need help, we must give them open doors and listening ears. Giving a child that *SAFETY NET* is seventh on the list of what kids need to grow well. Each item you provide will reduce your sense of guilt.

I believe in setting aside one evening every week for family togetherness time. It can be structured with projects, activities and reports, or just a night when everybody puts all else aside to play a game together. And, of course, it must include dessert. After all, what do you think the phrase "comfort food" means?

Family councils are also good. Especially as kids get older, they need to know that they can talk over problems with their parents. We need to convince our children that whatever help they need, we'll find it. If it's a psychologist, a doctor, whatever—we're in their corner and part of the team. Likewise, the one-on-one time I mentioned earlier must include opportunities for this kind of open discussion.

Just as adults feel more pressure today than in the past, so do kids. A list of kids' worries in past decades wouldn't begin to match the awesome fears on kids' worry lists today. Far beyond popularity and what-to-be-when-I-grow-up, are grave concerns about AIDS, the survival of our planet, gangs, murder, the splitting up of a kid's own family, and the burgeoning drug problem. Doctors report treating more juvenile cases of stress-related illness than ever before.

Children are growing up incredibly fast. I was appalled, not long ago, to hear of sixth graders dating. After one or two amusing thoughts of these children bicycling off into the sunset, or holding hands at Chuck E. Cheese, the more sobering thoughts took over. *These kids—these babies—could be having sex!* It's hard to imagine anything more tragic than a child losing innocence and childhood itself, thrust into a complicated, grown-up world before they've even signed their letters to Santa Claus. It feels like a form of robbery, only what was taken can never be restored.

Today's youngsters are dealing with custody battles, loneliness, materialism, and school pressures that make yesteryear look like utopia. Why do I launch into this tale of woe? Because it all spells insecurity for those poor kids. Here they are, pulled first one way then another—and today, more than ever before, kids need a safety net. There has to be somewhere, somebody, some set of arms, that can enfold these children and whisper that we're there. Everything will be okay. You are not alone. I love you.

Simply take a moment every month or so, and communicate this message. Sometimes an adolescent will pull away and "Aw, Mom"—but believe me, he'll reflect on your devotion to him when the path gets slippery and he needs that support.

Find out what issues trouble your child. Is he feeling stress you didn't even know about? Does he feel torn between two divorced people? Is he afraid for his safety in a violent world? Does he wonder what he's going to be someday? Talk it out. Ask him for his own ideas about how to solve—or at least deal with—the things that bother him. If he has some tools of his own to bring to the battle, his stress will diminish. If he knows that home is his refuge, despite the scariness of the world "out there," he'll always have that.

CHAPTER 10

Happy Air

Call it the mood of the household, the home atmosphere, whatever—it still comes down to the basic feeling you get when you walk through the door, which one of my boys called *HAPPY AIR*. Home should be a haven from the pressures outside, not a hotbox of conflict everybody dreads coming home to.

You've no doubt felt situations where tension in the air was so thick you could literally touch it. And conversely, you've probably been in other homes where you could just feel all the stress knots melting away (usually some wonderful scent was wafting through the air). Does this mean we all run out and buy potpourri to simmer on our stoves, or worse—bake a daily chocolate cake so the house will always smell like a fairy tale cottage made of sweets?

Not very realistic. But we can dramatically affect the mood of our house by controlling our *own* mood. It isn't baking up a batch of cookies or fluffy waffles (one non-cook friend of mine says the trouble with frozen waffles is that they never fit the grooves in the waffle irons, anyway!). It's creating a climate of encouragement and a welcoming spirit that permeates the house. Relax your eyebrows. Slow down. Take note and greet people as they walk in. Really mean it when you say you're glad that they're home.

And be happy, doggone it! A four-year study at the University of Washington showed that kids who perceived their parents as happy, cooperative and loving, also saw *themselves* that way. A big part of their self-esteem came from knowing that their parents had self-esteem! By taking occasional "being good to myself" breaks, you actually benefit your children. And you certainly should not feel guilty about *that*.

Another big factor in creating happy air is avoiding criticism. Children, inevitably, are going to make mistakes as they grow. If the truth be known, adults probably make more. But remember that your children are just *kids*. It's so hard to adjust our expectations, but it's so unfair if we don't. So many of us expect our children to act like adults; but this fills the air with pressure and leaves every kid stressed out. No wonder so many hide under headphones and in front of video screens.

Criticism is a cancer. It's a poisonous gas that fills the air and chokes out all the happiness molecules. Even if you open the windows and wave your arms (apologize), it hangs stubbornly there before you.

The best cure for criticism is to take a beat before you speak and ask yourself, "Is this a criticism—of anybody or anything?" If it is, find a way to rephrase it, or don't say it at all. If you try it for just one morning, or one day, you'll be surprised how often you stop and how quiet you become! Make it a game, so everyone can learn how to turn it off. If someone catches you being critical, put a nickel in the "grouch box." You'll either break the habit or the bank! And your kids will thrive and blossom like the giant kumquats you see in those seed catalogues. C'mon, you know what I mean. Suddenly, they'll feel loved and accepted. Their self-esteem will soar. They'll probably even conquer the things you were going to criticize.

But what if some criticism is needed? Correction can be

gentle, and can even result from simply asking questions. Instead of saying, "You are so sloppy I can't believe it—when are you going to learn how to pick up your clothes?" try, "You know, I feel so discouraged when I look at this room. What can be done about all the stuff on the floor?"

Sometimes we fall into the Fix Everything Trap. We want to buff and polish our loved ones raw. (I once heard a marriage lecturer say women would find greater results if they'd stop trying to make their husbands good, and simply try to make them happy. In many ways, the same applies to children.) Why don't we just take a deep breath, look at the big picture, and let some things slide? I don't mean the major stuff kids must do, like homework and being safe. I'm talking about parents who growl about the picky details—"I told you to comb your hair with water. Now go back and do it right, then you'll have to go to bed early tonight." Or "Stop dawdling at the pet store window. I said we have to leave now. And quit getting fingerprints all over the glass—someone has to clean that. (*swat!*)"

Parents who have hundreds of rules and serious punishments for the least infractions are sitting on powder kegs. I figure the kegs will explode somewhere around age thirteen. In an effort to yank their children right into successful adulthood, such parents allow no slack. They make ridiculous demands of children, allowing them no childhood at all.

Sometimes it helps just to say over and over to yourself, "He's only six years old. He's only six years old." There's plenty of time to learn some things; we often behave as if a stopwatch is running and we have to turn out perfect children by ten p.m.

We can also overburden our kids with all the extras we think we're "giving" them. You know the routine—you dash from school to piano to gymnastics to T-ball to art lessons, grab a quick bite and do homework as you eat, then dash to scouts. We're raising a generation of gerbils who only know how to run a treadmill. Twenty years from now, how many kids will remember a lazy afternoon, lying on the grass and watching the clouds go by? Would you really want your child to grow up without days like that?

You are creating your child's childhood memories right now. Let them be kids; let them get bored and think up something to do on their own instead of being entertained every minute. Give them a happy home. Give them plenty of chores, but lots of time to invent their own activities, too.

Happy Air is affected by our marital relationship, too. In today's world, when more than half of the marriages fail, it's not always easy to have the ideal environment in the home. Three tips can help.

First, keep the kids out of disputes as much as you can. For kids to watch arguments is only beneficial if arguments stay non-violent and end with a constructive solution and making-up period. You know best how you and your spouse fight, and whether your arguments tend to stay calm and have peaceful resolutions. If, like most couples, you don't "fight well," then for heaven's sake, don't fight in front of the kids. Realize that you two are not modeling the proper way to disagree, and take it to another room. Fight in private if you can't do it without alarming your children! It is the height of selfishness to ignore the little ones watching you while you blast away at each other.

Second, get help. Use free public counseling or whatever it takes to fix the marriage. Leave no stone unturned. Once you've had children, you owe it to them to do everything in your power to keep their world intact. Don't let a bad marriage flounder for years on end, scarring everybody involved. Divorce is not the quick and easy solution it appears to be. (If you thought you couldn't stand being married to him, wait 'til you try being divorced from him!) Work on the marriage, and expect to work hard. Recapture the original feelings that made you marry in the first place. This also models correct reactions for our children: When you have a problem, you don't just quit—you try to fix it.

Third, be brave enough to divorce if that truly is the only way to survive. If you or your children are being destroyed, find the strength to start over. Children must be sheltered from abuse.

Then, have the maturity to realize that no matter how he treated you, he is still their father and they need to find *some-thing* to love about him. Let them. Encourage them. Is it so bad to love someone imperfect? Isn't that an important lesson you want them to learn anyway? Besides, in time they will see his true colors, and their assessment will be theirs to own. They will trust their hunches much more if their conclusions aren't tainted by your input. So often when we criticize their father, we only make children want to defend him. We also set a poor example of forgiveness. And we get mired in blaming, and thus fail to grow ourselves.

Involving children in disputes, or using them as pawns or even messengers, places an unfair burden on kids whose lives are already unfair due to the disharmony in their home! Your children need you to make their lives easier, not more compli-cated. Hey—sometimes our problems are too tangled even for *us* to sort out. How can we expect youngsters to do it?

Save your anger for action that helps to solve the problem. Don't just vent around innocent children. You may think that showing all your feelings is honest and healthy, but it can be abusive to tender souls that need love and calmness. They need the assurance that both Mom and Dad love them. They didn't want their world to fall apart, and they need you to model strength for them.

Having been through a divorce myself, I know what I'm talking about. I have taught my two eldest sons to love freely, not feeling that they must choose sides. Don't expect children to be part of your support system. *You* are to be *theirs*.

CHAPTER 11

But Yes, But No

Point Number Nine: *CONSISTENCY AND FOLLOW-THROUGH*. I have to hand it to my husband; he is flawlessly consistent. He has never once shrugged and decided to go back on his word. (You know how easy it is; you're exhausted and you say, "Put that cookie back," but you're too tired to actually chase down the cookie-snatcher and enforce it.)

Fatigue is a big part of this, isn't it? Let's face it: It takes a ton of pure energy to raise kids. You can't just collapse on the sofa or take a nap. When kids are home, they need attention. Young ones need constant supervision for safety's sake, and the older ones need you at random moments which have to remain flexible.

We owe it to our families to keep our energy reserves replenished. If we allow jobs, friends, relatives, charities, etc., etc. to withdraw from our "energy savings" all day long, then when our children come to us, we're broke. We've spent all our energy on everybody else, and there are no reserves for our children or ourselves. It's like a bank advertising open hours, yet when customers arrive, it has no money to give them.

Picture yourself on an airplane, just before takeoff. The flight attendant is standing in the aisle, explaining safety procedures. You see the familiar yellow oxygen cup drop down, hanging from a clear plastic tube, and you listen as the flight attendant says something very important—something that applies to your whole life: "Put your own oxygen mask in place before you try to help your child." You can't give whatcha haven't got, ladies. You simply *must* replenish your reserves before you can hope to be an adequate mother, and give what your family needs from you.

I'm a firm believer in doing whatever it takes to replenish those reserves. For some (I've heard these rumors but can't personally testify to them), exercise is the rejuvenating key. Personally, I have often joked that sweat is the body's warning system, telling you to stop what you're doing immediately. But deep down, I know I'm wrong. Doctors tell us that exercise is one of the best ways to reduce stress and create a sense of renewed energy. When our health is good, our mental outlook (and patience!) really does improve.

Obviously, simply getting enough sleep is critical to having the energy it takes to rear children. And children themselves are usually the ones depriving us of it! However, we must persevere, moms. We must, if only on occasion, get to bed earlier or unplug the phone and sleep in later. Your health depends on it, and your family depends on you.

For others, a hot bath does the trick. It soothes out the stress knots, and you just might emerge completely refreshed and ready to tackle the parenting job again.

Hobbies, long walks, good books are all cures for some. I find lectures invigorating (I know others would be bored to tears, but hey. That difference of opinion is what makes life exciting). The point is to find what helps *you* renew and replenish, and then *do it*. To completely neglect yourself is to do a disservice to your family. And the same goes for dads.

Don't feel guilty taking a little time out for yourself. You are coming back to the job after a well-deserved vacation! You will be a better "employee" now. You cannot work at *any* job without a single break, ever. You simply must rest and renew. You see to it that kids have breaks from their routines, right? Do the same for yourself.

When you can keep from getting completely stressed out and hammered, you'll be better at enforcing rules. You'll be less likely to lose your temper, less likely to punish severely. Your thinking will be clearer so that punishments will fit crimes.

Once you eliminate fatigue, you can practice following through. I've found that if I take a minute before announcing my decision, I often take a softer line, one that's easier to enforce. Example. A child says, "Mommy, can we stop for ice cream?" My knee-jerk reaction is to say no. But if I repeat the question, I buy just enough time to think, "Hey—what would it hurt? We haven't done that in months." And I say, "Sure—good idea." Now, instead of dealing with a disappointed boy who's been told no without a good reason, I have a happy family where kids realize their questions are heard, not simply dismissed without any consideration. And if your answer is still no, you'll have a good reason that you won't feel guilty about. Just remember to stick with it firmly so the kids will learn that whining doesn't work.

Another help in learning how to follow through is to take one day (or a half-day) at a time, and vow to follow through for just that time period. Slowly you'll teach yourself how to do it for longer and longer periods, until it's your normal mode. It does require a different mind-set, and some of us don't come by this naturally. We can, however, learn the skill.

Today I see mothers at the playground who say, "Okay, Jessica, it's time to go now" about fifteen times in as many minutes before Jessica, who calls the shots and knows it, finally decides to leave. I used to be one of those whispering souls who was, frankly, stunned that my children didn't jump when I spoke. To my memory, it never occurred to me to defy my mother and start climbing the slide again. Yet there they were, fruit of my loins, doing exactly that. Partly not to create a scene, and partly to model kindness and sweetness, I used to repeat the same gentle suggestion until threats ensued, and the scene I had hoped to avoid was worse than ever.

Not so today. Today, I'm actually nicer and funnier and less upsetting than when I was afraid to upset my kids. What I now do is give a five-minute warning and then we leave. Can I admit to you that it is with no small amount of smug enjoyment that we march happily (happily, yet!) away as envious mothers stare? How-does-she-do-that is written all over their faces.

Is it the five-minute warning? No. I do that simply out of a burst of goodwill, and because one of my kids requested it and it seemed perfectly reasonable. After all, we all get engrossed in our activities, and a little notice is always helpful.

My husband simply taught me that when it's time to go, that's what you do. If the child will not cooperate, you bodily *take* him out of the park. You're not angry; you're just making sure you leave when you said you would. Who cares if it makes a scene? If you're worried about appearances, why would you choose to stay and look like a wheedling, whining, powerless excuse for a mother?

If he's too big or too fast, you make a factual announcement. "I'm going to the car. Now." Remind him of any consequences of disobedience. (Break a natural law and reap a consequence. Touch the iron, get a burn. Drive drunk and crash. Family laws should have consequences, too.) You can outline them some evening, or just before you arrive at the park. They should fit your own child. "If we spend too much time at the park, we'll have to . . . get up early to finish cleaning . . . do without some privilege . . . etc." And then enforce it!

When your child breaks a law and has to suffer the consequence, you don't enforce it with anger. You do it with genuine sadness. Just as you'd say, "Boy, I sure wish you hadn't picked up that broken glass. Cuts hurt, don't they?" You say, "What a shame you chose not to come in to dinner. I'll bet you're really hungry." It will be the last time he ignores your dinner call.

It's the same at the park. It's been years since I've even mentioned a consequence. At first, my kids had to learn that if they didn't mind me, they would lose a privilege. Today, my children have simply learned that when I say it's time to go, that's what we do.

It all goes back to saying what you mean, and meaning what you say. And you know what? It's also made my kids better at following through. When they say they'll do something, they do it because they've seen my husband and me follow through with the promises *we* have made.

Speaking of husbands, as every mother knows, they can make a world of difference in this whole topic of consistency and follow-through. If you're going to succeed in this category, you've got to be unified. You have to back each other up unfailingly. Even if you don't privately agree on every detail of discipline, you must come to an agreeable compromise on how to enforce the family rules. Once kids realize they can play one parent against the other, the only consistency you'll have is consistent trouble.

Knowing I'm the weaker of the two of us on disciplining the kids, my husband came up with a way to inject some guts, if you will, into my directives. He told the boys that when I tell them what to do, it's even more important than when he does. They stared at him, shocked.

"Your mother carried you for nine months and gave birth to you. She is my very best friend, and my girlfriend, too. If you hurt her feelings, you'll have to answer to me." They stared solemnly back at him. "If you don't obey your mother, then you'll not only have her punishment to deal with, you'll have mine."

You could just see the boys' eyes doubling their consequences as they listened. But you know what? They have never once tried to undermine either of us. We present a united front, and even if we disagree with each other in private—as is probably inevitable with any two people—we support each other's decisions regarding the children.

Some moms complain that while they're trying to enforce the rules, their husbands sit in some altered state a few feet away. Kids get away with sassing and disobedience, all under the nose of an unobjecting father. You may write in this book and circle these words: DAD IS YOUR JOB. I NEED YOU TO BACK ME UP. Then show it to him. Once you became parents, you took on a very distinct job. And one of those job descriptions is to work with a partner, not go solo or fall asleep at the wheel.

When one parent gives an answer or tells the child what to do and the child resists—or worse, gets sassy about it—the other should promise to leap to his or her feet and come down smack in front of the child. "Did you hear your mother?" (Tip: If a husband wants to know a new way to turn on his wife, he can practice the above example. Any woman in her right mind will feel such an outpouring of love and gratitude, her heart will skip several beats.) That feeling of support swells up like a golden, summer day. It also conveys great stability to the child, even though he may protest the direction he's being given. The knowledge that Mom and Dad are united is a solid foundation of tremendous security.

Single moms may appear to have it easier because they have no second opinion to figure in, but in fact their role is the toughest you can imagine, because nobody's there to back them up. I salute single moms who, I truly believe, bear the biggest burden in our society. They try so hard to be both parents, and it's hard enough just to be one.

But single moms can succeed, and any quick glance at

great inventors, statesmen, and world leaders reveals a surprising number of outstanding individuals who were raised without a father. Single mothers are definitely able to provide the consistency and follow-through children need. The trick is to juggle your schedule so that your children get *your* consistent influence rather than someone else's.

No mother has an easy assignment; that just isn't part of the job description. But it's possible. It's done successfully every day, by mothers just as imperfect as you think you are. You can be consistent. You can follow through. Determine that this is the kind of mother you are. Re-invent yourself, if you will. Say it ten times every time you look in the mirror. *I'm consistent. I'm the kind of mother who follows through.* You can re-program your brain and be stronger, turning a weakness into a strength.

Now. Go and teach your children to be like that. After all, isn't it quite likely that they, too, will be parents one day?

CHAPTER 12

Real Magic

Dr. Albert Schweitzer once said, "The only ones among you who will be really happy are those who have sought and found how to serve."[1] He knew what he was talking about.

This particular point is so important that I saved it for last, like a great dessert, so perhaps it will linger longest in your memory.

At first glance, *SERVICE* seems like rather boring good-deedism, and many parents gloss over teaching it. (Ironically, these are often the same people who are amazed at the demanding, greedy, disrespectful attitudes you see in youngsters today.) But if we fail to teach our children to serve others and one another, the only alternative is to encourage selfishness. Without serving others and caring for the needs of those around them, the easier path (i.e., "What's in it for me?") will be chosen. Such kids are blind to the less fortunate, unwilling to help someone in need, and usually will give only the bare minimum of effort—and then only when it pays off.

Kids who are allowed to fight and bicker continuously with their siblings, undermining and sabotaging one another at every opportunity, do not generally grow close in later life. When forced—yes, forced at first—to behave with kindness to their siblings, and to serve them, love does ultimately grow. Feelings do follow behavior.

---

1. Cited in *The Forbes Scrapbook of Thoughts on the Business of Life*, B.C. Forbes & Son Publishing Co., Inc., New York, 1968, p. 162.

In every divorce, selfishness is a factor. Maybe only in one person, maybe in both. But it was there. Selfish kids become selfish adults who find failed marriages, failed jobs, and child-rearing failures themselves. Look at the cases you know, and you'll see that this is true.

The only way to escape selfishness is to teach service and a basic love for humanity. When we teach our kids—usually by our own example—to care for the homeless, to take a meal to a widower, to do their brother's dishes when they know he has a big test tomorrow, to volunteer to clean up after a school activity, something startling happens.

These are the kids with self-esteem. If you learn only one thing from this book, let it be this: Service creates self-esteem. Memorize that and use it personally or with employees or your children or whomever. When children learn to serve, they don't just avoid laziness. They feel *important* because, frankly, they've just made themselves important to those they're serving. They come away feeling wonderful about themselves. They gain an edge over other kids in education, and, yes, they even gain recognition, which doesn't hurt.

Yeah, yeah, I know the old phrase, "Who cares what others think?" Well, I'll tell you who cares. University entrance examiners. Prospective employers. Potential spouses. Practically everybody is judged, if only a little, on reputation. Why not help your child get the reputation of being a kid who pitches in and knows how to make himself useful? Others will see him as the one who knows what's going on, and be drawn to him like a magnet. You automatically like a person with that kind of selfless caring, that kind of leadership, that kind of confidence. And best of all, he'll like himself.

One of the easiest ways to start children thinking of their brothers and sisters is to encourage them to plan surprises. Somehow the element of secrecy makes a game of it, and keeping sister out of the kitchen until you can do her dishes makes her final entrance worth all the trouble. "Now you can look!" a child will squeal. A little fanfare makes chores easier for everyone. Sister, too, learns to express appreciation, and maybe starts thinking up a surprise or two of her own. Love is definitely contagious.

A little boy might never want to make his brother's bed until you let him slap a ribbon bow on the pillow. Suddenly, it's a gift. A trip to the supermarket can teach compassion if you whisper, "Let's get Daddy's favorite ice cream and surprise him tonight!" Soon children realize that other-centeredness is much more fun than wanting things for yourself.

I frequently take meals to members of my church or neighborhood, when a new baby arrives, or a parent is too ill to fix dinner. And I am often chagrined, when I'm making something special, to hear one of my kids ask, "Is that for us or for someone else?" But they've caught the spirit of giving, and now they are often the first to suggest a certain dish they think someone would like.

One day I paid a visit to an elderly woman, simply because she was lonely, and two of my children wanted to come with me. Before we left—without a word of encouragement from me—they ran through the house to find the woman a suitable gift. One boy came back with a dollar bill and a dime (all he could find), and another gave her a small, but precious, toy car.

Some time ago Brandon, then six, asked me if there was any *real* magic. He had taken some magic classes after school, and so far everything had a trick to it. I was stumped. Rainbows came to mind. Rain, period. Cat's tongues cleaning cat fur. Caterpillars turning into butterflies. Falling in love. Magic was all around, but not the kind he meant.

Finally I smiled. "Giving away love, and finding more in its place." I thought he'd roll his eyes and groan, but instead he just thought. And then his eyes twinkled and he smiled. "Yeah," he said. He knew exactly what I meant.

SECTION THREE

Guiltbusters

CHAPTER 13

The Best Kind Of Mom

. . . doesn't exist. She truly doesn't. There is no singular, perfect, absolute best way to be. There are hundreds of styles of good mothering, every one of which can turn out terrific kids. And even the best mother you can think of would be better suited for some children than for others.

Some kids blossom best around a soft-spoken, gentle mother. Others like high-energy exuberance. Some kids need a tough, no-nonsense mom while a sensitive, lenient one is right for someone else. (And guess what? You usually get a mixed bag of children and have to treat each one differently anyway.)

I know a woman who is so flighty and irresponsible that I was sure her children would all turn out utterly incompetent, supported one day by my tax dollars. But guess what? They turned out fine. In fact, terrific. While I was judging from the sidelines, this woman was obviously doing something right; by hanging back, she taught her kids to pick up the slack, learn skills on their own, and become survivors. Do they resent her for making them do everything themselves? Not at all. She gave them one of the top ten you read about in the last section: a sense of achievement and real competence. So maybe their hems were stapled until they learned to sew, and they were late everywhere until they learned to drive themselves. Such details weren't her priority. But she *did* communicate love and delight in them, and they feel it back towards her.

On the other hand, don't we all know families who seem ideal, yet strangely enough, one or two kids have somehow gone haywire anyway? Think of a family you greatly admire, who has experienced this phenomenon. Mom and Dad are wonderful, loved by their relatives and neighbors, hailed in their work, and obeyed by all but *one* of their kids. Many parents who work hard to turn out well-adjusted children find that, despite their best efforts, children exercise their freedom anyway, and not always in the direction Mom and Dad had hoped.

Rather than blame themselves, these parents need to take solace in knowing they did their best. If you've really tried, then unwise choices are the *child's* fault, not yours. And don't look back at your mistakes as if these are to blame. EVERYBODY makes parenting goofs. Most kids still turn out all right. If one of yours rejects what you've tried to teach, go to sleep knowing you fulfilled your assignment. The ball is now in that child's court.

I am not saying this is easy, or that heartache can be shrugged away. But such parents MUST NOT beat themselves mentally for their children's adult choices. It's sad, and we mourn for the one we love, but sorrow does not have to be guilt.

Let me share an interesting theory with you. Embrace it or don't, but just mull it over. Some friends of mine believe that before we were born, we lived as spirits and all chose our families. Valiant, strong mothers chose difficult children because they knew they could offer more to that child than someone else could. They knew the child wouldn't be easy and would make mistakes, but they loved the child enough to say, "I volunteer to raise that one." Likewise, perhaps some of us chose difficult parents because they would force us to develop the traits we needed. It's an interesting thought, and gives pause when we wonder why on earth certain children are so headstrong.

Regardless of your personal beliefs, there is one truth that you need to remember, and it is that *there is no one perfect kind of parent who is guaranteed to raise perfect children.* Embrace your own individual style, make no apologies, and do your best. Don't try to be the same kind of parent someone else is. Your child may need you specifically, exactly the way you are. Find your own style of mothering, and enjoy being true to yourself. When a child is loved, it covers a host of unorthodox parenting methods.

I once had an excellent editor describe his work as hearing the author's true voice, and then keeping the author true to that voice. He didn't impose his own style onto the writer; he helped that writer bring out what was already there. Isn't that how we should encourage our children?

Renowned parenting expert Bruno Bettelheim said in *Parenting Magazine*, "The parent must not try to create the child he would like to have, but rather help the child develop—in his own good time—into what he wishes to be."

Along with letting our children be who they really are, we need to allow ourselves to be true to our own mothering styles, as well. And this sets a wonderful example for children of being comfortable with who we are. I once had a professor say, "Joni, you are the only woman I know who really loves being a woman and has no quarrel with it." I think he was simply seeing the enjoyment of life that comes when you finally stop scrambling to find yourself, and you like who you truly are.

Does this mean we stop trying to improve? Of course not. But we stop fretting that our style is all wrong. Except for the obvious abusive mothers, there's no such thing as a bad style.

So what kind of mom are you? I know one mother who,

despite having no ethnicity whatsoever, has somehow man-
aged to embrace all the adorable traits we associate with Italian
moms, Jewish moms, etc. Everyone around her laughs con-
stantly at her sharp wit, her insistence that everybody eat some
more, her shameless use of comedic guilt to get her kids to
behave, and her theatrical mannerisms. I was helping her
make a dinner salad one evening when the phone rang. She
answered, then in a moment said, "I go like this," and hung
up. Then, without missing a beat, she turned to me and said,
"That was just an exterminator company asking me what I do
about pests." At the same moment, her youngest son came into
the kitchen to ask for a quarter. "What do I look like—a Ready
Teller?" she asked him. "Well . . ." he said, cocking his head to
one side and squinting. Her humor was obviously rubbing off
on her kids.

I know another mom whose style is completely different.
Her patience seems to know no bounds. To my knowledge,
she has never raised her voice or complained of stress. She
smiles, she knits, she offers sympathetic glances. She reminds
me of Melanie in *Gone With the Wind*. She rarely speaks, but
when she does, her every word is kind or encouraging.
Granted, it's sometimes a little sleep-inducing to sit in her
quiet house and listen to the lulling tick of the clock; but just
as with the salad mom above, this one's children seem to be
doing great.

I guess I'm a playful mom. I love Disneyland even more
than my kids, and I'm the only one in the family who insists
there's a pot of gold at the end of the rainbow. I make up silly
songs (while my kids roll their eyes), I dance through the
house, and I count the days until I can wash the Thanksgiving
dishes and immediately put up the Christmas decorations.

Sometimes, with three boys and one rambunctious girl,
I've wondered if maybe they would have been better off with
a tomboy mom who appreciated sports and spiders rather than

pearls and roses. But then I look at how much they enjoy bringing me bouquets and stringing me necklaces, and I realize that they *want* their mom to be like I am. To artificially become rough and tumble would only confuse them.

On the rare occasions when I have forgotten to feign horror at the dripping fangs on a dinosaur one of them just drew, their faces register genuine disappointment. It's as if their definition of how I *am* has suddenly come under attack.

While I was telling the kids all about tarantulas on a family trip, my middle son rolled his eyes and whispered, "Miss Nature." But I've also seen him beam proudly as he tells his buddies about the science projects we do each morning.

Before the birth of my daughter, we had a family portrait made. (Incidentally, this is exactly like washing your car and then having it rain. Bob and I tried to have a fourth child and finally gave up, figuring we were just destined to be the remake of "My Three Sons." We even decided to go for the big family portrait. Naturally, as soon as we hung the picture on the wall, we became pregnant with Nicole. Lesson: Unless you're really, really, really sure, wait on the portrait!)

Anyway, the photographer had a hard time getting our then two-year-old son to smile. In very subdued style, she held out a stuffed toy and said, "Smile, Cassidy." She stood to the side of the camera and said again, "Smile, now." This went on for several minutes with no result.

Finally I pretended I was going to take Cassidy's thumb, then acted completely flabbergasted to discover that he had pulled it away. Thinking he'd pulled a fast one on Mommy, Cassidy dissolved into giggles.

After the shooting, Brandon climbed into the back seat of the car and said, "I'll bet that lady isn't a very good mom—she sure doesn't know how to make babies giggle." To Brandon, a good mom knows how to make babies giggle. Humor is such a big part of our home life that in Brandon's eyes, someone who can't elicit laughter seems unsuited for parenting. Another child—maybe the photographer's children—would find me silly or overly dramatic. The point is that all kinds of styles can work, and your own children will prefer your style because that's what they'll know. That's what will be true to you, and they in turn will feel comfortable being their true selves when they see that you are, too. If you're *not* satisfied, find a way to be.

I once heard a woman defend her decision not to have children by saying, "It doesn't stimulate my intellect to play Candyland all day." I thought to myself, "So DON'T play Candyland all day. Scoop up your child and go to a tide pool or a museum." If she's all that intellectual, surely she must have imagination enough to devise a stimulating diversion, right?

Be any kind of mom you wish. Whip up something intriguing in the kitchen. Or set up and time an obstacle course. Gather an igneous rock collection. Arrange a children's art display in your home. Set up a science lab, library, or learning center. Photograph your child's day and create picture books for the grandparents. Plant a garden with your child. Get and train a pet. Put on a puppet show or paint faces. Study astronomy, meteorology, journalism, advertising. Take her shopping and explain prices and values. Circle stocks in the *Wall Street Journal*, and mark their progress with your little investor. Exercise with your baby. Explore nature with him. Read books to him. Sell lemonade with him. (Obviously, you only choose the activities that fit your style—not all of them!)

Some moms hate kiddie crafts and pursuits. The most domestic thing about them is that they live in a house. Fine— not every mom has to wear an apron and greet her kids with homemade bread and honey. Some moms teach their kids to appreciate music and Shakespeare. Some build solar energy collectors with their kids. Some teach their children how to farm. Some moms explore other cultures, right in their own cities or on vacations. Some moms would spend all day out-doors if they could, and ought to. Some get involved in civic causes. Some moms like socializing and being around people. Others enjoy quiet pursuits or no pursuits at all.

Accept your style—soft-spoken, wise-cracking, task-dri-ven—whatever you are. Celebrate it and teach it to your child. He may still pick a different one, and that's all right. In fact, that's excellent! It shows that you gave him the confidence to be unique, and not to have to live in your shadow. You may never impart your love of opera to your child, but if you pro-ject satisfaction in your role as mother, you impart a sense of contentment. You'll teach your child to be happy with who he is, because *you* are content with who *you* are.

Find your own style, embrace it and love it, then live it.

CHAPTER 14

Honesty Is Not the Best Policy

My Uncle Frank gives public addresses on occasion, and one of his favorite speeches begins with the title of this chapter. "Honesty is not the best policy," he says. Then he pauses, leans in, and says, "It's the *only* policy." And, of course, he's absolutely right.

A great way to reduce your guilt is to take a good look at your life, and see if you're portraying a false image in any way. Any time you try to fake it, you'll feel guilty. Example. Do you conceal your temper in public, then release it upon your family within the privacy of your home? If you do, you'll feel guilty. Solution: Get a grip on your temper problem, so both your public and private images will match.

Another example. Do you hide your own mistakes so that your children will have a wonderful ideal in their mother? If so, you model perfectionism, hypocrisy, and an inability to admit being wrong sometimes. Solution: Be open and honest. Let kids learn from your errors, and let them learn that it's okay not to be perfect. Teach them how you've conquered various weaknesses.

Many of us behave dishonestly without labeling it as such. But you know what? It's still perpetrating a lie. And sooner or later, kids will find you out. This lesson was brought home to me on an excursion some time ago with my two eldest boys.

After weeks of letting the whole family binge on french fries, brownies, and soda pop, my guilt alarm went off and I humbly drove to a health food store to make amends by purchasing sunflower seeds and dried fruit for snacks. (Someday I'm going to get a phone call from a graduate student who's writing a paper on "Guilt as a Motivator," and she's going to use me as her prime source of material.)

Anyway, we walked past the produce department and into the grains section. Richie and Brandon were oohing and aahing as if in a museum of never-before-seen artifacts.

"Is this one birdseed?" Brandon (then age three) asked, pointing to a bin of winter wheat. I pretended that we were all making a joke and laughed a tinkly, little laugh, so that everyone around me would think, "That is a health-conscious family. Of *course* they know how wheat looks. That toddler is simply kidding his mother. He obviously has a highly developed sense of humor, no doubt the result of eating mung bean soup on Wednesday nights."

Richie, five, ran up to the dried banana chips and said, "Let's get these—these are *good!*" (He probably traded a Twinkie for some at kindergarten. The other kid, whose mother had painstakingly spared him exposure to even one granule of sugar, is probably at the supermarket this very minute, wondering why little Justin is crying for Twinkies and swearing up and down to her that he loves them.)

"Oh, I like those," I lied. "And bananas are a good source of potassium." That little factoid is probably the only one I can recall from junior high Home Ec class.

Brandon then pointed to the peanuts and said, rather brilliantly I thought, "Peanuts." Then Richie pointed to the split peas and said, "This is good for you. We don't want candy. Candy is yucky." (Okay—who body-snatched my kid?)

A woman nearby smiled—no, beamed—and said to me,

"Isn't that wonderful?"

Well, I am so transparent that I don't need to be X-rayed, but I tried to conceal my shock at Richie's sudden health-consciousness and said, "Yes, they're great kids." *And great kidders, I thought.* Or maybe they were just going along with Mom's game: Pretend You Know A Hill Of Soybeans About Nutrition. Had my fakery already caught on, and made my kids into equally phony shoppers?

Richie was now hamming it up, going on about how vegetables and fruits are so good for you, and how candy can make you sick. (In my own defense, I must admit to saying such things on rare occasions).

But I couldn't maintain the charade any longer. "Come on," I said, "You've never had a peanut in your life."

I rolled the cart over to the sunflower seeds, stuffed a little bag with them, and headed to the cashier. Tiny pouches of biodegradable cellophane held colorful vitamins which the kids immediately recognized as pill-shaped Gummy Bears, or so they shouted to the other shoppers. "Hey, can we get these?" Richie asked, picking up a carob candy bar. He sniffed it. "Hey—this one smells like sawdust!" Then Brandon had to smell it and announce to the store that it smelled exactly like the baths you have to take when you get chicken pox.

I decided our best move was to get the heck out of Dodge, so I pulled out my checkbook to get a head start. The cashier tapped on a little sign that said, "Checks dishonored."

"How do you dishonor a check—print bowling balls on it?" I asked. Everyone in the Soy Set just stared grimly at me, but my KoolAid Kids thought it was funny enough to repeat over and over, so as we were leaving, I tousled their hair and said, "C'mon—let's go to Mrs. Fields'."

So I'm not Nancy Nutrition every minute. The honest truth is that I do let my kids eat raw cookie dough. (When I recently told Brandon that some people actually don't like raw cookie dough, he gasped, "That should be a *commandment!*") The fact is, we're a family who likes its desserts—and to pretend that I Osterize carrot juice for them every day would be to live a lie. (Some time ago a girlfriend gave me a plaque that reads, "Life is Uncertain: Eat Dessert First.") Do I feel guilty for lacing their lives with sugar plums? Not at all. I do give my kids a balanced, healthful diet—I really do—and they rarely even miss school or catch colds. Frankly, they seem smarter and more robust than their carob counterparts. What *would* make me feel guilty is if I were trying to live a double standard.

Sometimes we even lie to ourselves. I once saw a mom in Toys R Us who was getting to the end of her rope. (You know that familiar end that you see around the kids' bedtime every day?) Anyway, her fuse was nearly spent, and as her kids were whining and grabbing and making her gray, she gritted her teeth and snarled at them, "I said we are leaving *now*." Her voice was so shrill that you knew she'd been announcing their departure for at least twenty minutes already.

A little moppet in the front of the cart looked up at her and said, "You mad, Mommy?"

"No, I am not mad," the woman hissed, lying literally through her teeth. "Mommy does not get mad."

Well! What a crock, right? And the little girl's face looked as puzzled as it should have. Clearly this woman *was* angry, but by saying that she wasn't, she's teaching dishonesty to her kids. Now the little toddler is wondering, "How can she look so angry, and not be?" How can the daughter learn to read this woman—or anyone?

My three-year-old, Nicole, occasionally asks me the same question, usually after I have reprimanded one of her brothers in no uncertain terms. "You angry, Mommy?" she asks.

"You bet I am," I say. Then I tell her why. Sometimes I tell her I feel angry when one child deliberately torments another. These are appropriate reasons for being angry, and I want her to realize that it's okay to feel anger. Is it okay to lose my temper and explode? No. Is it okay to get angry over trivia? No. Is it okay to tell her I'm happy when I'm obviously not? No. But I owe her an honest answer about why my eyebrows are scrunching together. It ain't 'cause it's my birthday!

We need to be absolutely honest with our children, because trust is so delicate a thing. If children feel you have deceived them, you have just toppled their idol: you. They may never again believe you with such pure faith and trust. They will also learn that it's okay to misrepresent the facts to accomplish certain ends—a terribly misguided lesson.

Kids encounter enough duplicity and falseness in the world outside your home. They need to know, deep in their hearts, that Mom has never lied to them, and that, of all people, they can trust you. Besides, showing emotion appropriate to the situation is healthy. To do otherwise confuses and bends their personalities in unhealthy ways. Would you want a child who laughs at another's misfortune? Or one who feels sad when she should feel happy? Or a child who denies that she's angry when she has good reason to be?

We then need to show our children what *actions* we take. If we're angry, do we channel that energy into positive steps that bring the results we want? Or do we explode and overreact? Do we pace and mutter to no avail, just letting bad situations get worse? Or do we teach our children how to solve problems?

Sometimes the deception is more serious than simply denying that you are angry. If you've already concealed something you shouldn't have, come clean. Ask their forgiveness, and let them know they would have yours in the same situation. A lie ignored still grows.

Be an honest mom, free of pretense, and you'll also be free of guilt.

CHAPTER 15

You Are Not Your Mother

Despite hearing that you are just like your mother (if that bothers you), or hearing that you'll never be quite like your mother (if you wish you could), the simple truth is that we're all individuals.

Sometimes I'll call to Bob, and then—he *claims*—he answers and I start walking the other way, mumbling. "What's that, Coralee?" he'll ask. Coralee is my mother, and she is notorious for calling your name and then speaking to you so softly that you have to go to her and stand right in front of her to hear the message. I bristle at the comparison, though there are other qualities of my mother's I only wish I had.

But let's assume, falsely of course, that I do have this annoying habit. I'm STILL not my mother. I am entirely different in disposition, personality, age, number of children, and sex of children than she was during her childrearing days. And you aren't your mother, either.

Why do I make this point? Because *despite your similarities*, in order to erase any guilt, you must see yourself as separate from your own upbringing. You are not condemned to repeat your parents' mistakes, and you are not a terrible mother if you see wonderful things your mother did that you can't equal. You are simply different. Hopefully, you will come to realize that you're actually much better.

We know so much more about how to raise children these days. Each succeeding generation is luckier than the last, as they are born to a society that—in general—is better equipped for the job. And aren't you? Don't you read more articles and books about parenting than your mother did? Don't moms talk amongst themselves more than ever about the decisions we so carefully make in our children's behalf? (Earlier, I pointed out that all this close scrutiny can contribute to our guilt—and it can. But it can also benefit our kids if we resist panic and keep a level head.)

Not only that, but each year we learn more as human beings—science, medicine, education, the arts, politics. We gather more knowledge and bring to our parenting the experiences and information of centuries.

Children today are safer from being molested, because awareness about social dangers is much greater. I don't believe that there's more incest, molestation, and abuse than ever before (look how many adults are in therapy for this right now); I think we're finally talking about it now, and warning our children about it. These crimes are no longer kept so secret. And that's great. Souls are literally being saved from emotional scarring and torment.

And look how different fathers are today! Dads are far more involved than they were in previous decades. Kids can only benefit from all this progress.

And you are part of that! You are a special mom, giving your gifts at a wonderful time, when so much is available to help you and your child. When I hear people say they wouldn't want to bring children into such a horrible world, I feel renewed vigor for my task—I'm raising kids who'll be part of the *solution!* Aren't you, too?

You bet you are. Your kids will benefit from your dedication to your job as mom. How do I know you're that extraordinary?

Because an uncaring mother wouldn't have picked up this book. The very fact that you're reading about it should tell you that you're a pretty neat mom.

And aren't you excited to see what kinds of parents your own children will be someday? Don't you hope they'll be even better at it than you are? Isn't it precisely right to expect each succeeding generation to improve upon the last one? Isn't that what learning from mistakes is all about? In many ways, you're probably a much better mother than your own mom.

Does that mean we fault our mothers and join the whiny group of mom-blamers who refuse to take responsibility for their own choices, pinning everything on a dysfunctional family? You've heard them. "I would have gone to college if my mom had encouraged me more." (So why aren't you enrolled in evening classes right now?) "My mom was always fat, and I just learned bad eating habits." (What—she's force-feeding you even today? Make a diet plan!) "My mom always criticized me, and that's why I have low self-esteem." (Pick yourself up and finish the parenting job she didn't—vow to be a better mother than she was.)

We all had imperfect mothers, and it's *okay*. If you didn't like how you turned out, stop blaming your mom and take charge. Re-invent yourself. But don't get mired looking back and crying over what's done. Realize that just maybe, she did the very best she could. Maybe her *own* mother wasn't so terrific, and she came into the job without much training. Maybe she was in an unhappy marriage and you never knew it. Maybe she had always wanted to be a ballerina. She was a little girl once, with dreams just like you had. She was human.

Regardless, forgive her and move on. BE THE MOM YOU ALWAYS WISHED YOU COULD HAVE HAD. Instead of raising another dissatisfied customer, be different! Start over! You really can do it.

And stop comparing yourself to mothers on the other end

of the spectrum, who appear to be absolutely perfect. Except in those rare cases of genuinely ego-inflated mothers, we'll always come out of a comparison on the short end of the stick. We tend to be self-critical and forget our strengths.

One mother, whom I'll call Kelly, used to make just such a comparison. Kelly was a yeller, and her neighbor was the most soft-spoken woman she'd ever seen. This woman was so quiet she actually whispered most of the time. Every time Kelly had to yell out the window for her kids to stop swatting the cat, or pulling each other's hair, she'd glance over to her neighbor's yard, where Mrs. Whisper always handled things quietly.

"How does she do that?" Kelly used to think. Then one day her son and some of his friends were throwing a baseball against Mrs. Whisper's house. Bam! Bam! Bam! Kelly was about to yell out the window for them to knock it off, when she saw Mrs. Whisper come out of her house. "I'm going to watch what she does," Kelly thought.

Sure enough, her neighbor bent over and whispered something to Kelly's son. The boys immediately left, and began walking towards the ballpark. Mrs. Whisper went back inside. Kelly darted out a side door and caught up to the boys. "What did she say to you?" she asked her son, eager to hear the magic secret.

He shrugged. "Well, she said that if we threw the baseball against her house one more time, she was going to take it and put it down the garbage disposal."

So you see? Things are not always as they seem!

Don't assume that everyone else is holding it together better than you are. Be confident! If nothing else, know this: You are endowed with a mothering instinct for your own child specifically. Doctors, neighbors, relatives may all have terrific ideas; but not one of them has your motherly inspiration. A mother is always first to know and insist on a solution if her child has a problem that no one else can detect. Likewise, when others think something's wrong but you have a gut-level feeling that your child is just fine, he is. There is no other mother for your children but you. Unlike any job or career you've ever had, in this one you absolutely cannot be replaced.

Ignore intrusive advice, especially advice that just doesn't ring true. Trust your hunches and ignore old wives' tales. No matter how you parent, you'll meet half a dozen people willing to tell you to do it another way. Expect this, and shrug it off. The opinions of the masses are for pin-striped guys on Madison Avenue who want to sell us a truckload of floor wax. Those guys *need* public opinion. You do not.

So accept the fact that you're not your mom (or your neighbor or your sister), and stop beating yourself for the traits you see in them which seem invisible in you. You are terrific in your own way. (Besides, they probably see you in the same glowing light that you see them!)

A short time ago, I was comparing my own childhood (seen in retrospect through several thicknesses of rose-colored glass) to the childhoods my sons are having. It seemed as if my childhood was much more Norman Rockwell—I biked all over the small town where I lived, I played with the dozen kids in my neighborhood, and no one ever hovered at the curb when I went trick-or-treating, just to make sure I was safe.

At the time I was doing all this comparing, we lived in Los Angeles, and it was very different from my old hometown. At least for my sons, there definitely wasn't the same Huck Finn flavor to their early years that I'd had. I drove them to their piano lessons and baseball games, I telephoned the mothers of their friends to arrange play dates, and I'd call the police if they were wandering the streets alone at night—Halloween or no Halloween.

Did I live in a crime-filled ghetto? No. I simply lived in a major city in modern times. Kidnappings and crimes happen so quickly, and I wasn't the only mother I'd see living in her car as she chauffeured the kids back and forth all day. Most neighborhoods today aren't full of kids as they used to be, and the sound of a screen door slamming because your children ran out the door to play with Jimmy seems to be a sound of the past.

I said to one girlfriend recently, "We're the new homeless. Have you seen your house in the daylight during the last six months? You drive the kids to school, run errands, take the baby to Mommy and Me class, stop by the library, post office and dry cleaners, pick up one child, take him to violin, pick up the other, take him to scouts, go back and get the first child, take him to a birthday party, get the scouts boy and take him to soccer, pick up the birthday child, take him—"

"You're absolutely right," she laughed. "I am never, ever home anymore. I just live in my car."

My mother sees the difference today, too. "You never ran me ragged like that," she says. She's right. When she was raising my sister and me, kids could make their own entertainment, and could walk or bike to their activities. "Be home by dinnertime," was her parting counsel as we ran gleefully off to play. It was safe, it was simple. It was yesterday.

In the middle of this nostalgia and melancholy over my boys having to play by appointment, I could also see some joy and delight in the opportunities they had that I didn't. We took advantage of the rich offerings of a large city. My kids were exposed to a wider variety of people, arts, cultures, and excursions than one could ever dream of in a small town. Sheer numbers of schools allowed me to select from a smorgasbord of options. And my regret over not having a neighborhood full of kids to play with was easily outweighed by the fact that my kids got to *choose* their friends, instead of getting stuck with what could be a block full of bullies. Last, I suppose it goes without saying that my Heidi-style childhood of thawing out my frozen fingers after walking the honest-to-goodness two miles through the snow each day, would never win over our own moderate California.

You are not your mother, and your childhood neighborhood is probably not the same one (even if it *is* the same one) that your children are experiencing. DIFFERENT IS OKAY. But you can enhance their childhoods by giving them their own set of fond memories. Preserve the traditions you loved, and create new ones you wish you could have had. Tailor their memories to them, not to you. Take advantage of the climate, the culture, and the pluses where you are now. Accept the way you're mothering, and know that you're doing all you can. Your children will grow up with the same warm reflections of their childhoods that you had. To them, "the wonderful way it used to be" will be the way it is right now. They'll wish it for their children just as you long to give them what you happily remember.

Not long ago, at Christmastime, I was tucking my two eldest boys into bed. I suddenly remembered my own happy anticipation of Christmas and the huge, billowing snowdrifts that always piled up against the door on Christmas morning. Sunlight glistened on the icy twigs and branches, making every tree a spectacle in crystal lace. Suddenly I could taste the snow, feel my cold fingers in their mittens, and see my breath turning to steam before me. My eyes grew moist. "I wish you boys could know the white Christmases I remember," I said.

And then one of the boys asked, "What does it look like when it's snowing?" It was all I could do to hold back the tears. Here were my precious babies, being raised in Los Angeles and arguing on the freeway about whether a passing limousine is a stretch or not (at which moment I vowed to move back to the Rocky Mountains, by the way).

I took a deep breath and tried to describe the snap in the air, the incredible lightness of a single snowflake, the seven names for various kinds of snow we had, and the way you could look up into the sky and see stars of pure white, descending forever and ever. Soon my sons fell asleep, the lemon tree outside their window mottling moonlit shadows across their beds. I sighed. I could not give them my childhood.

But you know what? My boys had happy childhoods all their own. They had wild geese arriving for the winter. They had beaches, deserts, and snow skiing within one day if they wanted it. They had fresh fruit growing in their yard, year-round. They had big-city excitement and cultural events at their fingertips. They had French classes from pre-kinder-garten on, in a wonderful private school that even taught alge-bra in the fourth grade. They had Disneyland and Knotts Berry Farm. They had bougainvillea cascading over our walls, in pinks so brilliant you'd think it was a floral sunset. They had *warm* campouts. They didn't have my childhood, and they didn't have my mother. They have their own childhoods and they have me. All in all, I think they got a pretty good deal.

CHAPTER 16

Keeping Up With the Johnnys

One of the best guiltbusters I know is to escape the competition trap. Parents today seem compelled to out-do each other in every conceivable arena. They are defining their own personal value by their children's achievements, and they'll stop at nothing to engage in this one-upmanship. Not only does this hurt the individuals engaging in it, but it gives our children a twisted sense of priorities. It teaches them to seek applause, to let all their happiness be in another's keeping. It also puts them under tremendous pressure.

Parents who compete will never escape guilt, because that's guilt for good reason. Your conscience is—or should be—grabbing you by the arm and saying, "Stop!"

You know where I see a perfect little microcosm of this phenomenon? In kids' birthday parties.

The *Los Angeles Times* asked me to write an article about this, and by the time I had collected my startling information, I called it "Pin the Tail on the Parent." I was amazed at the lengths we parents would go to, throwing a bash for our babies.

"She roller skates. She plays the harmonica. She even exhibits her original artwork in a number of galleries. She is the cutest elephant!" one party director told me. She was talking about one of their hottest, and undoubtedly largest, party items.

I learned of one family that spent $80,000 on a party featuring a complete carnival with roller coaster and a circus with trained elephants (they passed on the Madonna impersonator and the dogs that jump rope and sing). It used to be that the only parents who rented a carousel for their children's birthday parties were people like Joan Crawford, whose kids then grew up and wrote fascinating books about them. But such extravagance is no longer limited to celebrities.

Is guilt one reason why party companies were telling me their business had quadrupled? Are busy parents trying to make up for neglecting their kids all year by throwing elaborate celebrations of their youngsters' births? And then, not to be outdone, are the other parents joining in to hire yodelers and jugglers, too?

Partly, it could be that the baby boomers have larger family incomes than previous moms and dads, and they're willing to slice off a more generous hunk to the party entrepreneurs, who'll gladly take $100,000 and more to create the illusion that your child is having fun at his birthday party. Business cards that used to list gymnastics, computer, or music lessons now boast "PARTIES!" as well. The predictable chaos of gatherings at fast-food restaurants has been replaced by Las Vegas hopefuls who come to your home in a candycane rickshaw.

The yuppy puppy no longer merely pins a tail on a donkey. She gets sawed in half by someone like Doug Henning. Who does your child adore? Big Bird? Power Rangers? Bart Simpson? Barney? Whoever it is, there is someone who can impersonate him. You can fill your yard with llamas, camels, clowns, mimes, bag-pipers, and a petting farm zoo. One company will bring in a scarlet macaw with a five-foot wing span.

I personally went to one party where children could enjoy an inflatable castle moon bounce, a magician, a puppet show, button-making, shirt-painting, toys of all descriptions, and a menu that ranged from barbecued beef to shrimp on ice. It was truly staggering.

One mother I spoke to said her daughter's second birthday was the worst day of her life because it was too overwhelming. Parents have allowed peer pressure to catapult a simple little celebration of a child's birth into an extravaganza with a bigger budget than some movies.

When I was growing up, you dropped clothespins into a Mason jar, or you threw a raw egg back and forth. Sometimes there were scavenger hunts or spook alleys, but most of the games' ingredients came out of a kitchen drawer. Like all my playmates, I loved those parties and relished the laughter and chatter of noisy kids who knew how to make their own fun.

I don't know if your neighborhood has fallen into the Party Pit like mine has, but I don't see parties like that anymore. Every birthday looks like the wild invention of Dr. Seuss, and I think we can place a good bit of blame on guilt.

Working mothers who no longer have time to plan the party themselves, or who see this as an opportunity to display newfound wealth, are setting a whole new standard. And full-time parents, too, are getting scooped up in the dragnet, competing with the new state of the party.

I confess I fell under the spending spell myself. When my eldest son turned two, I had the brainstorm (more like a power outage) of a fiesta theme, complete with sombreros for all the toddlers, Spanish dancers, a huge buffet of Mexican food which only the parents really ate, and a candy-filled piñata. All I can say, in retrospect, is that anyone who gives a bat to a two-year-old deserves whatever happens to their windows and parakeets.

Today, I will no longer consider trading in the donkey tails for donkey rides. Godzilla may meet Mikey at some parties, but not in my backyard. Today, my kids plan their own creative parties. Richie's ninth was a Nintendo obstacle course at the park, where he had his friends fight their way past Kupa—Bob—to the princess—Me—who guarded their treasure—party favors. Brandon's seventh was a pirate theme with buried treasure in sand—simple, inexpensive, and best of all, outdoors.

We must simply refuse to compete. When you do stop comparing your children to others, and stop competing with other parents, you begin to truly savor parenthood. You relish the uniqueness of your children and your home life. You fall in love with the lifestyle you're providing, and the family you are. You finally feel calm and unhurried as you move confidently through the actions that you, alone, have chosen.

But it takes constant vigilance. Bob caught me slipping on this one some time ago. We were sitting at a Cub Scout pack meeting, as one boy was being strewn with awards like a Christmas tree. His belt and shirt were covered with every conceivable emblem, patch, and bead. I craned my neck to see what on earth a kid could accomplish that I hadn't yet steered Richie toward.

Bob pretended to be wiping something off my shirt. "Just brushing off the envy," he said. "You're starting to ooze." I grinned; he was right. Generous traces of my over-achiever childhood are still creeping into the way I approach the Cub Scout manual and its array of tasks. I still remember holding the book up to Bob and saying with complete astonishment, "Why, I'd have these done in a week! I'd go right down the list and check off every one of these projects. I don't see why Richie—"

"Isn't you?" Bob sometimes has this way of hitting the nail squarely on the head. "Let him go at his own rate," he said. "Be glad he doesn't have to compete with everyone else."

Alas, he was right. Richie feels confident and happy without scrambling to be first all the time. It's actually a healthier approach than mine. That tendency to be a ham and show-off and finish in first place is really not a terribly attractive trait of mine, I must admit. And it has been a personal struggle to put aside that need to compete as I've parented our children. But when I've been able to do it right, I've felt a tremendous burden lifted. And a good bit of guilt evaporates in the process. You can do it, too.

Let me tell you the story of Ryan. Ryan's parents, Vic and Toni, were worried that Ryan wasn't learning to speak soon enough. So they did what any good parents would do: they brought in a ringer. Peter, the little boy next door, was just twenty months old and was already rattling off long sentences in crisp, clear syllables you rarely hear even on the nightly news broadcasts. Maybe inviting him over would prompt Ryan to learn a word or two.

Until this moment, the best Ryan had offered was a muffled "Grup!" whenever he pointed at anything. Peter, on the other hand, could easily name toys, books, people, cars, and even say the Pledge of Allegiance without a hitch.

The big evening arrived, along with Peter and his parents. The moms and dads sat down with bowls of ice cream, and the boys disappeared into Ryan's room for a while. Envisioning their son as the willing protege of their neighbor, Vic and Toni waited excitedly for the medicine to take.

And sure enough, the boys played quite happily for over an hour, returning at last with several of Ryan's toys in tow. Peter ran gleefully to his father, pointed at Ryan's truck and exclaimed, "Grup!"

What Ryan lacked in linguistics, he made up for in leadership.

Yet comparisons are almost irresistible. Watch the eyes of new parents as they push their infant in a stroller and see another similar family. Both sets of parents stare seriously down at the other's little bundle. For what? To see if their child is as big? as bright-eyed? as adorable? as well-dressed? as happy?

Mothers congregate at parks, "mommy and me" classes, postnatal workouts, and nursery school parties to give their babies new social experiences, right? Well, partly. But also, and sometimes more importantly, to compare notes. Has Jessica started singing to you yet? Does Michael still sleep in a diaper? Has your son been accepted to that private school? Does Amy still carry that blanket around?

To the degree that this interchange improves our ability to raise children, I'm all for it. We can't all read every book and article, and it's comforting to know that others share our struggles and often solve them. But too often mothers simply brag. "Jason's climbing out of his crib already," they say, their hospital suitcases barely unpacked. "I can't believe Maria; she does equations faster than my calculator!" "Did you hear Kyle? He just rattles off his address and phone number like you or I would." "Courtney's composing music now."

I once wrote an article about this and mentioned a friend of mine, Hiromi, whose five-year-old daughter was just entering school then. She bumped into another woman whose five-year-old was writing her numerals up to twenty. Hiromi dashed home, filled with the panic we all know so well, sat her daughter down and said, "Here's a pen. Write to twenty!" Her daughter just blinked.

So many of us worry that our child will fall behind, that we will fail as parents to provide the options and opportunities that make them successful and happy. Our children will be scholastic cripples, and it will all be our fault.

But let's look at this business of comparing our children to those who seem more "gifted." Nancy Rader, Ph.D., a developmental psychologist at Ithaca College in Ithaca, New York, says the problem goes beyond healthy pride in your child and a natural concern that he not fall behind his peers. Many parents, she observes, "use their child as a step up the ladder of status, to fulfill the parents' needs rather than the child's. Creating a genius is the new status."[2]

Joel Cooper, Ph.D., chairman of the psychology department at Princeton University, agrees. "They are measuring their own worth as a parent and as a human being when they do this. Finding that their child is first or best is verification of their own worth. Likewise, if their child does something wrong, it means they, as parents, have failed."

Do kids ever pick up on our anxiety? "The child is going to grow up feeling he must succeed to earn love," Rader says. And Cooper points to research showing that by age seven or eight, "kids become acutely aware. It can make children feel very unworthy if they fall short." Cooper would like schools and social services to watch for kids at risk, who come from highly competitive homes. He says parents need to learn that their own worth is not based on their child's achievements. And comparing children can do damage—not to mention creating guilt!

Yet despite the experts' warnings not to worry if little Matthew isn't walking at sixteen months when your sister's kid was winning marathons at half that age, we persist. We see a tiny baby in a shopping cart, methodically counting her mother's purchases, and we gasp. Is the whole world going "super" on us?

Stop and think about these so-called "geniuses" for a moment. Haven't you seen a countless number of pre-school readers who still can't open a door? Do you continue to marvel at the child with perfect pitch who, at age seven, still won't share her toys? Are you overlooking the fact that the Little League pitching wonderboy usually picks a fight whenever he loses?

I'm not saying all gifted children have a hole somewhere;

---

2. This statement was recorded during a telephone interview. Subsequent statements for which print sources are not cited were also made during telephone interviews.

like most parents, I'm hoping my kids turn out to be superior across the board. What I'm saying is that too often we examine one isolated area of achievement and then *assume* that if our child lacks such brilliance, all hope is lost and failure is inevitable. We forget that children grow in spurts and starts: today's nature girl may be tomorrow's bookworm. Their development is spotty, and performance that is low in one area may skyrocket the next year.

The truth is, we all have talents and weaknesses. Your child probably got about as big a serving of pluses and minuses as every other kid on earth. We simply have to stop looking at the handful of abilities so publicly applauded and realize that our children excel in their own ways.

Too many parents look at the traditional fields of excellence and cringe when their child doesn't march out ahead in these areas. They look at reading, math, music, science, logic and analysis, spatial reasoning, art, physical coordination, and mechanical ability. And these are all wonderful areas in which to excel. But your child can still succeed, can still have a joyous life, can even become a millionaire—if that's important—without those as strong suits. In fact, being pushed and prodded to achieve can backfire, according to Rader. "It robs the child of self-motivation," she observes, and she has seen it lead to rebellion, depression, and even attempted suicide. "That's an extreme case," she says, "but it is a danger."

Start thinking, for a moment, about less easily measured virtues. How many mothers would gladly trade their teenager's athletic prowess for the ability to resist negative peer pressure? Plenty. What about the quality of leadership? Somewhere, someday, I predict, little Ryan will get his "grup" into the dictionary and have half the country using it daily, because that's the kind of charismatic child he is.

Why don't we trumpet the virtues of honesty, forgiveness, spirituality, integrity, generosity, empathy, and self-discipline?

Many an adult can take college classes in the academic subjects missed during childhood. But where can you learn creativity and optimism if you didn't learn it in your youth? How can you catch up on patience or sense of humor? How much harder will it be to develop self-esteem, an even temper, intuition, and humility? Will marriages and careers stand patiently in the wings while some of us work on sensitivity, flexibility, maturity, and a good memory? I don't know a single adult who learned the value of hard work as a grown-up. If it doesn't sink in during childhood, it almost never will. And why isn't there a special award for the common sense that Voltaire reminds us is not so common?

Linguistic geniuses, math whizzes and natural dancers may possess all these characteristics, too. I'd love to see every child develop inner strengths as well as a few proficiencies in the traditional arenas.

But the biggest battle doesn't seem to be getting children to do well. It's to get their parents to stop comparing and relax. Cooper reminds us that "children develop at different rates. Not seeing a talent at a particular time doesn't mean it won't happen later. And everyone is good at something, even just pleasing people with a great smile."

When Richie was three, he had not yet drawn people with distinguishable hands and feet, or even heads and bodies. His nursery school paintings looked pretty much like impressionistic . . . impressions. So it was with some surprise that I sat down to watch him color and heard him say, "I'm going to draw a picture of Jeffrey and then give it to him."

Gulp. Would Jeffrey's mother be insulted to discover that her son bears a strong resemblance to a gravy stain? I took a breath and leaned in to watch. Near the top of the page Richie had scrawled some green zigzags. "What's that?" I asked.

"That's his hair."

"But doesn't Jeffrey have blond hair?"

"Yep. He already has blond, so I'm giving him green."

It made wonderful sense to me, and we proudly took the painting to Jeffrey's house. His mother seemed delighted, then showed us Jeffrey's latest drawing. It looked like the stuff I drew in the fourth grade! Eyes, nose, mouth, fingers, clothing—a very obvious portrait of a *person*. I was all but speechless.

On the way home, I brooded about her son's obvious artistic aptitude. Maybe I should sit and drill Richie on cylinders and cones. Maybe I should encourage him to color inside the lines instead of all over the page. Maybe I should go out and hire a private art tutor.

"I liked giving Jeffrey his picture," Richie said, interrupting my deep thought.

"Huh?" I turned to my son and then had one of those wonderful "light bulb" experiences: Richie had enjoyed creating a gift and presenting it to his friend! Richie loves that kid and has already mastered the fine art of generosity!

I thought about Jeffrey's pictures—beautiful, yes, but none given away. I thought about how often Richie would put a compassionate arm around another child to comfort him. I thought about how, when we pulled onto a busy street and another driver would shake his fist at us, Richie would say, "Wasn't that nice of him to let us in? And he *waved* at us!"

It was too early to tell where Richie's strengths would lie. He could design rockets or dresses—I couldn't guess then. But already I could see his achievements in spheres beyond measurement, in ways that no test could ever tally. He's gifted, all right, if only because he is giving.

And I, at last, learned to put aside comparisons that kept me from seeing how very important green hair could be.

(As an interesting postscript, you should know that Richie's school entered his artwork to compete with twelve-year-olds in the California State Fair when Richie was in first grade. He won third place).

CHAPTER 17

Working with Dad
(in the picture and out)

If you have one of those marvelous husbands whose favorite role is Father, much of your battle is won, and much of your guilt should already be diminished.

These are the men who would never miss a child's parent-teacher conference, school play, or ball game. They help you put the kids to bed, they wrestle and tickle with the kids one minute, then have a loving heart-to-heart chat with them the next. They back you up when it comes to discipline, they diaper, they share all parenting responsibilities completely.

And while once rare creatures, their numbers are increasing. Such dads are to be saluted and cherished, encouraged at every step—just as good moms should be. Homes where fathers put the family first are homes that turn out stable, happy children who grow into stable, happy adults.

To the degree that we can make fatherhood a rewarding and fulfilling option (as opposed to staying late at the office), we should try. Just as good fathers try to ease the burdens on Mom, so should we try to make their lives easier, too. Let's face it: Parenting is a tough job, and there are trying times and bad days when spaghetti is hanging from the ceiling, teenagers are slamming doors, toddlers are throwing tantrums, and youngsters are throwing up *almost* in the toilet. When you're the only Mom or Pop home at those times, you need your counterpart to come through the door and rather than unload about *their* tough day, simply pitch in and help you through yours.

Too often we take our partners for granted, and we forget the strokes and appreciation that keeps kind acts forthcoming. Yes, we should parent well because it's our responsibility. But on a practical level, we're all human; we give more and strive harder when we know that our efforts are appreciated.

Parents get so little thanks for what they do; if it comes at all it's usually deferred twenty or thirty years, and that's why we need to show gratitude to each other along the way. It's a two-way street. I once heard a speaker say, "A father's place is in the home whenever he can be." He went on to tell men that the family (first the wife, then the kids) should be their top priority. When a man leaves the home to earn a living, it should be because he must, in order to support the family unit. It shouldn't be because work is an escape, or because his career occupies a loftier spot in his heart than the children do. I'd say the same goes for both parents.

Sometimes, when the father isn't pulling his share, we as wives are guilty of contributing to his perception that he's on the outside looking in. How many times have you heard women say their husband is "babysitting the kids tonight" when in fact, Dad is watching his own children, the same as you would if *he* had to attend a meeting? Would you ever describe yourself as "babysitting" your own children?

Other times, because we feel we do it best or know the situation better, we inadvertently push our husbands aside as we care for sick children, buy their party gifts, help with homework, etc. Many of us need to lovingly involve our husbands and, yes, lean on them. You love best the people you've sacrificed for and served, so guess who benefits most when you allow your husband to be more involved? The kids! They'll build a wonderful closeness with their fathers if we stop pushing the men out of the picture.

Now, I realize that not all men are inclined to participate. Or rather, they are otherwise inclined—on a La-Z-Boy with a bowl of popcorn, for example. Let's discuss this type of man for a minute.

What do you do when Dad isn't helping you to create a united front? What do you do when you can't count on him to support you . . . or to even be there at all?

Before you build a stockpile of resentment which will color the very words you choose, have a heart-to-heart talk with him. After explaining the problem you see and the solution you think would work, *listen.* Ask questions. Maybe fatherhood scares him. If the baffling popularity of the movie "Field of Dreams" is any indication, most guys were raised by some pretty ineffective dads. Perhaps your husband, afraid to be as inept and non-demonstrative as his own dad was, is simply pulling back, scared to death that he'll somehow screw it up.

It may not make sense to you. Logically, he should try even harder to not repeat his father's mistakes, right? But emotionally, he's simply holding an empty bag. Some dads don't have one single tool in that sack of parenting supplies. They never experienced their dads setting a good example, so now they have no clue how to do it. All they know is that parenting is awesome stuff. They also see, gratefully, that they've married a woman who knows more about babies and kids than they do. So—logic again—they step aside and let a pro do the job.

We need to assure men that they *do* have the necessary skills. Every "outside" skill can translate into a parenting skill. I'm not saying we coddle these guys or give them false praise. But we can work with them and show them that it's not the Mission Impossible they think it is. Often, when we recoil from a job and describe it as unappealing, it's because we fear we wouldn't be good at it. If you can just get him to try for a short time, he'll feel the rewards; and what he thought he'd have no interest in will suddenly be dear to his heart. It's like that with kids, especially: You love those you serve.

And, of course, any such effort from a husband should be richly rewarded. Let him feel like the two of you are part of the same team. You're not his tutor. You're not his employee. You are his sweetheart. You're united. Remember your wedding ceremony? C'mon—*live* those words!

In a short time, the reluctant father will realize he didn't have so much to fear, after all. Even when he goofs, he'll see that life goes on, and goes on pretty well. Finally, if you continue to support his efforts, he'll grow into the job beautifully.

Some dads hold back from involved parenting because, subconsciously, they actually resent the children. Now, don't immediately think, "Oh, that's not my husband. He loves our kids." Yes, he says the words, and he provides for them to some degree. But see if this picture fits your relationship:

Did your husband lose you as his lover when you became a mother? Many couples struggle with getting the romance back when a demanding, colicky baby has entered their lives. New mothers seek help all the time, trying to understand what happened to their sex drive. Did the arrival of a baby mean the departure of your love life?

If so, *some* dads harbor secret resentment that all this new responsibility and expense has no up side. The wife is preoccupied, she's exhausted, she's frustrated that she's not back to her old weight yet. It's a real downer, in some ways!

These couples need to talk about the problem. You need to become his sweetheart again. He needs to help you with the demands of a new baby so you won't *be* so exhausted. It isn't that he doesn't love the children. It's just that he sees them as competing with him for your energy and attention.

You must put the marriage first. The best parenting advice

I ever heard was to go on a date once a week with your spouse. And it works! You let the kids know where they stand (certainly they're important, but the married couple is the Number One relationship in the house). You also let each other know where you stand. Your husband will know he's first in your heart, and you'll feel attractive and courted again. Sound old-fashioned? I think it sounds fantastic.

Parenting is much easier when you're in love with your partner. You both need to reaffirm that you haven't just formed a cold partnership devoted only to raising kids, but that the spark is still there. Your commitment is for keeps. Splitting up is not an option. You are both determined to work through any problems that may arise. (And problems *always* arise. That's normal.)

Your weekly dates will let the two of you renew your communication skills, too. You'll be able to discuss feelings, work out compromises, and even talk about parenting strategies for crises without being in the middle of one!

Okay, what if the dad you're dealing with is your ex-husband? This opens up a whole new can of worms, and in many cases you know exactly who the Chief Worm is. If you have mutual respect and a decent working relationship, count your blessings. Your kids will benefit from both their parents' efforts. But if there are hostilities, underminings or manipulations, you have to take strong action to protect your children. Make this your top priority. Getting even, saving face, and all those other personal agenda items need to be shelved. Forget the couples issues, and do whatever it takes to raise happy children who feel loved by all. By doing so, you'll know in your heart that you're a good mother. And a good mother has a good self-image. She won't even worry about such petty pursuits as getting even with somebody. Confident people don't get even. They get a life.

If, despite your best efforts, you have not been able to

work well with your ex-husband, you must look at your options. (Continuing to let each side simmer, by the way, is not a smart option.) Here they are:

Court orders. If the situation is destructive enough to the children, do not hesitate to take whatever measures you must to protect them. Get a restraining order against violent or abusive fathers. You are your child's only advocate, their only hope for protection and safety. You cannot put them at risk.

Humble Pie. Often hostilities continue because of pride and egotism. Let's say he ran off with another woman. Get on with your life and be glad that you're rid of him. Let's say he said terrible things about you to your friends. Live a life that proves him wrong. People aren't stupid. Okay, *some* people are stupid . . . but why would you want *them* for your friends?

Don't model grudge-holding or revenge for your kids. Smile and be the bigger person. If you've made some mistakes yourself, apologize. Do all you can to smooth over the relationship, and don't be preoccupied with who is right. Hanging onto ancient history will cripple your growth and increase your guilt, and your anger will hold you back from being the mom you could be. Put your kids first and your own agenda last.

Negotiate. Make every effort to work with your ex-husband, even if he's extremely difficult. Try to discuss household chores, music practice, sports participation, discipline, and school activities that should ideally match in each home. The more in harmony you can be, and the more alike the homes are, the more secure your children will feel and the less adjustment they'll have as they travel back and forth.

Set the example. Remember, as a mother, yours will be the primary influence. Even if you can't control the damage you feel is done when the children visit their father, at least you can do your best when they're under *your* roof. Maintain your rules and lifestyle. Don't compete on your ex-husband's level. If he spoils the kids with toys, don't play that game. If you give love and genuine caring, there will be no contest. Kids know where our hearts are. If you had to pour your heart out to someone, would you pick a mother who always listened and cared, or a dad who just bought you things? While toys and trips are momentary fun, your love will give them the real, enduring kind of joy and the sense of acceptance that outlasts any toy.

CHAPTER EIGHTEEN

Now That's Funny

Around the middle of August, most moms freak out. I'm serious. Summer, which oddly has a positive reputation, turns into a battleground between bored kids who need to go back to school, and mothers who are ready to drive them there. Yesterday.

Now, not *all* moms endure this. Some moms love summer and wish their kids could be home all the time. Believe me, these are women who simply lucked out and got easy kids (or few kids). This doesn't mean you love your children any less, or are a worse mother. You just have kids who like driving you crazy. The other mom doesn't. No big deal.

And, let's admit it. We all have super days when our kids *are* perfect angels. We wish we could prolong that feeling forever, and snuggle and tickle and play with our babies right into eternity.

But back to reality. Let's say you fall into the category of the mother who is going bonkers, and who thinks straitjackets should definitely come in size 2T. She is certain that summer vacation lasts entirely too long, and her "fairytale" life looks like the one where the bears keep finding that "someone has been eating my porridge, sitting in my chair, and sleeping in my bed."

I have been blessed with the opportunity to experiment with various solutions to this problem, and I have found only one that really works. Happily, it works marvelously well. And it is humor.

I know a mother who had one of those grocery store experiences which all mothers are destined to have (and repeat), wherein you go in for a soda pop case, and you come out with a mental case. Her four-year-old son decided to have a tantrum—not just a "sit on the floor and wail" tantrum, but a "run screaming up and down the aisles" tantrum. A doozy. After trying to no avail to catch this wild child, she finally strolled into another aisle and, exchanging stunned glances with another woman, shouted, "Where's the mother?"

The other lady nodded her approval and moved along. My friend then hid behind a display rack and nabbed the little villain on his next pass through produce.

Truly, though parenting is the toughest and most demanding job on the planet, it is unquestionably the funniest, too. And to drag through the job without ever realizing this, is to have missed the whole movie.

We need to lighten up and laugh now and then. There are too many serious elements already; why pass up those hilarious moments when we can best enjoy our job?

Here's what you do. Keep a list of all the funny things that happen (there are usually several every week). Include funny lines your toddler says, goofy mistakes that even you make, all of it. Every few months, type it up and share it with grandparents. Put copies in photo albums. Reread it and be amazed at how much you would have forgotten if you hadn't written it down.

You'll see your children's personalities unfold as never before. It's even better than photos for capturing the real essence of your child. But best of all, it will make you start *looking* for the humor in life. You'll approach each day expecting to have another entry in your ongoing journal. I keep a little notepad in my purse, and I've even pulled off the road to write down something I'm afraid I'll otherwise forget. It has become priceless. And funny.

One of my favorite incidents happened just last week. Our family, except for six-year-old Cassidy, was gathered in the family room where we were all watching a movie. Suddenly, Cassidy burst into the room wearing a little army helmet that he had wedged onto his head, a plastic breast shield, a Ninja belt, and a bullet strap. Pointing two Super Soaker squirt guns at us, he shouted, "Nobody freeze!" Uh, okay.

When he was two, my eldest son set a record for curiosity. I was singing in a church choir of women when he escaped his pew, ran down the aisles, and up onto the stand where we were singing. As though the whole thing were premeditated, he marched right down the row of women and lifted each one's skirt. (And some of these were elderly women wearing girdles, I might add). You could tell where he was in the row by the sudden soprano notes being belted out. Forte. By the time I saw the problem, he had exposed the undercover work of at least seven women.

And when Richie was three, and would say Ys for Ls, he gave us a family story that still gets quoted today. We had been hunting for a parking spot, and finally found one close to the store. "We are so lucky," I told him as I pulled in.

"Yes," he said. "We are so yucky." This is the same child who once pulled me into the kitchen and said, "Let me show you what I'm sorry for doing."

We even quote Nicole, who is giving us funny lines at age three. On a recent walk around the neighborhood, she saw a dead squirrel and said, "Ouchy! Sorry!"

On a visit to his uncle's house, Brandon, then three, couldn't wait to snuggle with the new puppy. As the dog napped, Brandon put his head down against the dog's tummy, but soon jumped up soaking wet. That little dog had gotten him good—all over his face and head. We all laughed until we thought we'd split, and even Brandon thought it was funny.

This is the child who, when I invited Santa Claus to come to our house for an early visit, immediately recognized this bearded man as an intruder and shot him with a squirt gun, square in the eye. He and his older brother dashed away from us on a tour of Philadelphia once, and were in the process of ringing the Liberty Bell when a guard screamed "Stop!" and we dashed to find our boys trying to make the evening news. I could just see the headlines: "LIBERTY BELL CRACKS IN HALF, Negligent Parents Scolded by President."

About a year ago, Brandon's room had passed the tolerable limit for "displayed collectibles," shall we say, and we insisted that he clean it before he went to bed. Early the next morning, he frantically burst into our bedroom shouting, "Someone took all my stuff!" We reminded him that he had put it all away the night before, and a sheepish ten-year-old went back to bed.

I was driving Richie home from scouts not long ago, and asked him if he'd like to play a game when we got home. I was bragging about how I was going to beat him, when I heard snoring in the back seat. Suddenly he snorted and said, "Oh— what a coincidence. We were both dreaming at the same time."

A recent line of Cassidy's: "Next time we have raspberries with whipped cream, would you please not put any raspberries in mine?"

And when Cassidy was running through the house after breaking free from a playful wrestling hold, he crowed, "I'm free! I'm free!" To which his three-year-old sister retorted, hands on her hips, "No; I'M free."

When he was four, Cassidy once sneezed all over my dinner plate. "Cassidy!" I said, "Why didn't you cover your mouth?" He looked at me in all seriousness and said, "I didn't want to get my hand wet."

A few months ago, Richie lost some privileges, as teenagers tend to do when they disobey. I asked, "Do you feel this punishment is unwarranted?" You should have seen the surprised look on his face. "OF COURSE it's unwanted," he said.

And when Brandon once asked me what kind of cream I was putting on my face, I told him it was wrinkle cream. "Why would you want wrinkles?" he asked.

Last Halloween, I watched as Brandon stuffed his trick-or-treat bag into a hiding place. "Don't eat any of my candy," he instructed me. And then, "You're the only one I have to tell."

Richie, too, has taken on an occasional parental tone. When I asked his opinion about a parenting topic I was to discuss on my weekly radio segments, Richie said, "If I tell you, you'll never learn."

Some time ago, Cassidy told me that he's faster than a Ferrari and faster than a porch. And evidently I have been setting a speed record or two myself lately, because this same child recently said, "Slow down—you're walking like a waitress!"

When Richie was about five, he came up to me while I was jotting down some notes at my desk. He asked me if parents die first, or if their children do. Oh boy, I thought, a big discussion on death coming up. Very carefully I decided not to arouse his worries—but not to lie, either—and I said, "Well, usually the parents die first, because they're older." Then I watched to see how this would sink in. Richie stared at my hands for a second. Then he said, "Well, can I have that pen when you die?"

Cassidy came in from sledding last winter, and Bob asked him how he got the scratch on his forehead. Cassidy said, "Why—do you see a tree mark?"

Not long ago, Richie suggested that I become a contestant on the game show JEOPARDY! "Seriously, Mom," he said, "You know all the answers." Well, I have no intention to humiliate myself on national television (I do it enough locally), but I can certainly enjoy the idea that I actually have a teenager who thinks his mom is smart. He also made the recent suggestion that I should have my own cooking show. What a kid! That boy is going to have one lucky wife someday, as she rakes in the world's greatest compliments!

But, speaking of that game show, it must have been on Richie's mind about a month ago when he got into the car and said, "Brandon, move your legs." Trying to get him to ask more politely, I said, "Richie, would you please put that in the form of a question?" and Richie immediately said, "Okay. What is, 'Brandon, move your legs'?"

Even tattles can be funny. Nicole recently tattled that her tummy had all her cookies. And Cassidy reported that "Richie keeps wiping my spit on me." He also recently complained that his brothers were saying things that bother him.

"Like what?" I asked.

"Like, 'Get out of my room,'" Cassidy said.

Only last week, while Cassidy and Nicole were snuggling in my bed before heading off to their own rooms, Cassidy said, "This is the best time ever! I feel like I'm going to burst! I feel like going crazy!"

And one of my all-time favorites happened the last time Cassidy cleaned his room. "Wow," I said as I surveyed the good job he had done. "You really have a gift for cleaning your room." Excitedly, he made a victory fist, bent his elbow and said, "Yes!" Then he looked up at me and said, "What is it?"

You have these sorts of stories, too. Look for them, enjoy them, save them. And they will save your sanity over and over again.

SECTION FOUR
Plugging the Holes

CHAPTER 19

Love Means Definitely Having To Say You're Sorry

You've just had an argument with your husband. It was a misunderstanding, but your feelings are still hurt. Now you can hear him in the kitchen unloading the dishwasher. He rubbed your shoulders a few minutes ago. Whenever he seems to be sorry, he bustles around doing *things* to show you he's sorry.

So what's the problem? Maybe nothing, and his behavior speaks your language perfectly. You can tell he's sorry by how he's acting.

But most women need something more. They need to hear the words "I'm sorry," plain and simple.

Some people have a tough time saying they're sorry. *I* do! I don't *like* admitting I was wrong. It feels awful. But I simply have to say it, to make sure my loved ones know that I am. And I do it to teach my kids that Mommy isn't perfect, and needs forgiveness now and then, too. I don't want my children to grow up unable to say the words, simply because they've never heard them. What could be more ironic than a mother forcing her children to "tell Jeffrey you're sorry," when she herself never does it?

And don't we like to hear it when we've been wronged? It

may pain the sayer, but it heals the hearer. It wraps things up and gives us closure, so we can say, "I forgive you." It's a chance to turn wrong into right. We all make mistakes, but we don't have to make yet another by refusing to apologize. Then you have *two* mistakes!

This is one of the best ways to plug the holes and eliminate guilt. If you need to apologize to your children for something, don't wait another minute. If you need to forgive them for something, don't wait another minute. If you refuse to forgive someone, or refuse to take responsibility for a mistake you've made, you will never escape the guilt trap. Deep inside, you'll know you're running from unfinished business.

Sometimes the person you need to forgive is yourself. Give yourself permission to be imperfect. Watch yourself make changes and not be the way you used to be. Determine to do it, then let go. By not forgiving yourself for past mistakes, you keep yourself from growing, finding true happiness, and being a good mother.

Okay, it's often hard to apologize. What can you do? First, separate yourself from your behavior. Think, "I am basically a good person. This is just something I did this time. It does not define my total self. The action was bad, but *I* am not bad."

Your mistakes give you an opportunity to show your children that change and learning go on all through our lives. Show your child, by your own example, how a person demonstrates regret and perseverance in conquering a weakness. Show him that genuine regret is followed by resolve; we actually *change* something about ourselves.

Some people have an easy time apologizing—too easy, perhaps. They think a quick "Sorry!" will erase every hurt as they clumsily plunge through life. We need to be careful of assuming that every offense can be so easily brushed off. They can't. Don't you still hurt because of something said or done to you long ago? Aren't we all, really, the walking wounded, unable to forget the cruelty and teasing we encountered as kids? Yet many of those events were probably apologized for. Still, the hurt was too great to balance out one tiny apology.

To be guilt-free, we don't have to be mistake-free. But we do need to guard against the gigantic mistakes that *no* apology can erase. Sometimes the wounding is too great, the blood loss too immense, for any apology to cover it all. This risk is a serious one, and one which we should guard against with vigilance. Precious little souls have come into our homes, trusting in us completely. We cannot shatter their security, then expect an apology to heal them. Trust is not so easily rebuilt.

But if we treat our children as the precious and delicate treasures they really are, then we need not feel guilt. Our occasional missteps can and will be forgiven. "Fess up" when you goof. Admit your mistake, and tell your child how you plan to be different in the future. Then *show* them. Let your kid be proud of having such a determined mom who really does what she says she'll do. Children will want to be exactly like that, and emulate your great example. They don't want a perfect mom; they just want a mom who is doing her best.

Sometimes we've hurt our children's feelings and they don't want to forgive us right away. That's okay. Give them time. But don't fall into the trap of begging and buying in order to be forgiven. Don't promise outings or treats "if you'll forgive me." Forgiveness is about love and trust. It has nothing to do with extraneous rewards. If you teach your child that the "sinner" needs to grovel, plead, and shower the offended party with gifts, then when your child makes a mistake, he'll wonder how on earth he can ever make it up to you.

Let the apology fit the crime. If your crime is large, you'll need to demonstrate a changed heart over a long period of time. But if we're talking about the minor errors we all make from time to time, let a sincere and loving apology stand. Then it's up to your child to find forgiveness in his own heart.

My husband once did something that upset me horribly. It embarrassed me and made me feel uncared for. Through tears of hurt I explained this to him, and even though it may have seemed petty to someone else, it was important to me. Bob agreed never to do it again. And then, six months later, the same thing happened! This time, I was more crushed by his betrayal of a promise than by the embarrassing thing itself. Now I was not only hurting, I was angry. I even told him I wasn't sure I could forgive him this time.

And you know what? He said something I've never forgotten. "That's not an option!" he said. "You *have* to forgive me. What are we going to have—one of those awful marriages where people collect resentments and just live out their lives as old people who don't really like one another? You *have* to forgive me!"

And he was pleading to be forgiven, too. We both knew the kind of marriage we wanted—the kind in the top one per cent. We believe our marriage is for eternity, and we both want to fight with all we've got to protect it. So I had to look inside my heart. I had to realize that my marriage and my love for this man was more important than the occasional personal offense, of which there are dozens in every good marriage.

I looked him in the eye, and I knew immediately that he was right. If we were going to have the kind of marriage worth having, I had to forgive him. And I did.

Through example, we can teach our children the joy of both apologizing and forgiving. You need to be able to do both, not only to have a happy family, but to grow and "get on with life" as an individual. The goal of every good parent is to raise an independent adult. Our children cannot be independent and free adults if, as children, they are left alone to harbor resentments and grudges, or to justify and make excuses for their own mistakes. By stepping in and correcting them, you will shrink your guilt down to just about zippo.

CHAPTER 20

Goals: Take It Slow

Most people have no clue about how to set goals. They give it a stab every New Year's, then blow it by February, concluding that they're just not people who succeed, and live with that disappointment the rest of the year—until the next year, when they can reconfirm this negative opinion all over again.

Here's how to climb out of that rut and do it right.

First, pick one tiny goal. One. Tiny. Not a list. Not a goal that takes a lifetime to reach. Just something small and easy. Break the cycle of failing at goals, and adopt the self-definition that you are a person who *does* achieve her goals. You simply are. That's one of your talents. And you can prove it, because you *did* come to a full stop at every red light today. You *did* balance your checkbook. You *did* floss. (Or pick any other small, easy goal like that).

Now branch out a little. A *little*. Set another goal that's a tiny bit larger, or one that takes a bit more time. Keep going like this, in baby steps.

And don't expect your progress chart to be one perfect, diagonal line going up. Just like a hospital chart, there will be zigzags on that upward journey. Relax. Even if you take two steps forward and one back, you're still making headway.

Keep on without giving up, and you will soon be the envy

of all your friends. You will be achieving all kinds of things! Your world will become more organized (and thus more relaxing), and your own mood in dealing with your children will soften and become flexible, because you'll be in charge. You'll have a plan and you'll know it. When things don't get done, you won't worry because you know that, basically, you are a person who reaches her goals. It's one of your talents.

And when you do reach those mini-milestones, reward yourself! No, do not go on a guilt-inducing food binge or a budget-busting shopping spree. C'mon—a great goal-reacher like you knows better than that. But you can certainly give yourself rewards that feel good and continue to boost your motivation. Even a good book, a long-distance call to a friend, or a bubble bath can feel like a reward. And attach another reward to your next hurdle, so you'll have a carrot to reach for again.

Now, let's apply all of this to real life. First of all, you can't get rid of guilt if you're not doing a good job. This book is not about going happily along the wrong path and not worrying about it. You can't be *guilt*-free and also *care*-free. Giving less than your best will continue to elicit guilty, shameful feelings. Only when you really believe you're a terrific mom can you get rid of the guilt.

Nobody can reform and conquer all their weaknesses in one afternoon. But the good news is that you can still be a terrific mom and be imperfect. All you need to do is to be on the right track.

So, first, take an inventory. What do you do that's superb? Be honest; there will be many items on this list. Now, where could you use some improvement? Some moms wish they pushed their kids less, yelled less, had more patience, didn't work so much, could get their kids to stop sassing or watching so much TV. Whatever you think your problem areas are, they belong here.

Got that list? Okay. Now ask yourself if these worries are

realistic and necessary. Are you really as bad as you think? Perhaps not, and perhaps you're just being too hard on yourself. Get your husband's opinion. See what your kids think. I was never so stunned in my life as when I, who worried that I was the strictest, meanest mother in town, discovered that my kids view me as a pushover! (So then I worried about *that*.)

Now, take your list and focus on just *one* area where you'd like to improve. List everything you can think of that might help you be better in that area. Then pick *just one* thing off that list and do it for two weeks. Voilà! You are on your way to self-mastery. Just knowing you're on the right track will release tons of guilt steam. This is the start of plugging any holes that you find, and you do it hole by hole until you've conquered them all. This is not a race. Remember, direction is much more important than speed.

The key to reaching goals is to split them apart into tiny, manageable pieces. Don't try to eat the whole cake in one bite. Just proceed a crumb at a time, and you really will get there.

Maybe, when you are brutally honest with yourself, you'll discover that there's a weakness keeping you from being a good mother that you simply cannot conquer by yourself. You may need professional help. There are more problems than just the obvious ones, too. We all think of "moms at risk" as being alcoholic, drug-addicted, welfare-addicted, or violent. But plenty of moms simply need help working through anger, believing in themselves, organizing their career plans, or simply learning how to parent! There is no shame in correcting a problem and seeking help; there is only shame in refusing to get that help when it is needed and available. It's kind of like that saying, "The crime is not people who can't read; it's people who can but don't."

Once you *are* touching all the bases, or working toward that goal, pat yourself on the back and *stop worrying*! Banish guilt from your life—you've earned the right to do it!

CHAPTER 21

Sixty Seconds That Can Save Your Children

You've been reading about lots of ways to become guilt-free, and now I'm going to give you the fastest way to feel your guilt level actually dropping.

It's the sixty-second hug.

I wrote a magazine article once, explaining how this technique works for couples. But it works just as well for children.

When was the last time you hugged your kids—or anybody—for a solid minute without stopping? Sound silly? Well, it has actually been documented to reduce stress and establish greater trust and intimacy.

Sex therapists invented it to help couples re-establish closeness and break down the barriers we tend to build in our marriages. They prescribe it for couples to do every day, even using an egg timer, if necessary, to make the hug last a full minute.

Why are those sixty seconds so important? Because an elongated hug does some things that a regular hug doesn't. Dr. James Elias, Director of the Search Clinic in Sherman Oaks, California, says, "If you're held in physical contact long enough, certain physiological changes occur. Breathing becomes synchronized, nervousness is reduced, and it has a tranquilizing, calming effect. Heat changes have been filmed and you can see how the body warms. *Both* bodies warm. Studies have shown that if there's a relationship involved, it happens even faster."

Howard Ruppel, Jr., a social psychologist at the University of Iowa, is another therapist who advocates the sixty-second hug. "Time plays an important role," he says. "Research shows that quality and duration affect the outcome of the interaction. This is true in working with juries, teams, any group." Short hugs simply don't have the "relevance and dimension," he says. "Occasional squeeze hugs get to the point where it means very little. In our society we really don't understand the power of touch."

Elias also says it reduces contention and helps resolve conflicts. "It's hard to stay angry when you have a touching bond. The hug doesn't resolve the issues, but it establishes the relationship more closely so that you can. And it can reduce the importance of certain issues, too," diffusing them before they can become arguments. "The greater the bonding, the more vulnerability people risk."

Doctor of Education Leah Schaefer uses hug therapy in her practice in New York. She says, "When an argument is finished, people can demonstrate passage of their anger by holding each other."

While couples sometimes have a hard time getting started, feel silly, and need to let themselves go, children do not. They instinctively love to be held, and almost always welcome a sixty-second hug. Sometimes people feel self-conscious and giggle at first; sometimes they even fall over! But after about thirty seconds, all the wisecracks die down, and that's when you start to feel the magic.

It isn't a quick fix for every problem in your home. But it certainly sets a stage of trust and warmth so that issues *can* be ironed out with your kids, and intimate feelings shared. And what parent truly cannot find sixty seconds each day to give their children?

Trust and closeness are automatic dividends for families who hug this way, and when you know you're providing that, your guilt will drop right before your eyes!

CHAPTER 22

Taking Control

Some time ago I was at a local park, where families had gathered with picnic blankets to enjoy a summer concert. One boy was running about, across other people's blankets, upsetting jugs of lemonade, stepping on people's food and knocking over drinks. There was absolutely no difference between his behavior, and say, the behavior of an unleashed Labrador. His parents sat on lawn chairs and occasionally called out, "Don't do that, honey. Come back here." But he ignored them, and they merely watched as he continued to wreak havoc on the crowd.

Of all the trends I see these days, the one that most disturbs me is the lack of respect and discipline I see in young people. I see parents trying to be friends and forgetting to be parents. I see kids running wild, uncorrected, and usually followed by a simpering mom who shrugs as if to say, "Oh, well, what can you do? Kids!"

It's as if the monkeys are running the zoo.

To be free of guilt, you have to be in control. If your child is in control, you will never feel guilt-free because a little voice inside you will keep whispering that you need to take over the reins. It's not right and it's not natural for kids to run the show. They don't have enough judgment yet. That's why they HAVE parents!

Our children understand that our family is definitely not a democracy. "You want democracy, run for congress," I tell them. Mom and Dad call the shots. Does this mean we never listen to their side of an issue or let them choose which pants to buy? Of course not. I ask their opinions about nearly everything. But when it comes down to rules and decisions, Mom and Dad are not to be challenged. And despite kids' maneuverings to have more power, they really feel unsettled if they get it. They are too young for such weighty responsibility. They actually like—and need—the security of reasonable (not arbitrary) limits around them.

We can learn a great lesson from shepherds. The shepherd's job is basically to keep the sheep alive. He would be very irresponsible if he let the sheep climb through the fence and eat the clover that would make them sick, right? So no matter how much the sheep bleat and push to get through the fence, the shepherd has to be firm. Is he worried about being popular with the sheep? No way. Likewise, you shouldn't worry about all your decisions being popular with your children. Worry about being right, not popular.

When we moved to Iowa, our then twelve-year-old, Richie, got wind of a wonderful rumor: Because they're often needed to drive tractors, fourteen-year-olds can get learner's driving permits in this state.

"Can I get a learner's permit when I'm fourteen?" he asked.

"Sure," I said, "If you can find a parent fool enough to let you."

Richie snarled through a smile, and I knew that while he was hoping to get my permission, he also knew that I cared about his safety, and I wasn't going to blow with the winds of a lenient law if I didn't feel it was good for my family.

Am I saying that to take control you need to become an authoritarian whip cracker? No. You just need to be firm and consistent. In fact, by being firm and consistent, you avoid the trap of being too lenient for too long and then exploding with pent-up frustration.

You never want to make so many demands of a child (or give so many commands) that they feel bossed, burdened, and broken. One trick is to grant a privilege every time you have to place a restriction. "No, you can't have a popsicle now, just before dinner, but you can have one after." Or, "No, you can't invite Ashley over tonight, but see if she can come on Saturday."

When you approach the rules this way, your children will see you as a reasonable person who is not just full of no's and don'ts. They will be more willing to obey when you have to say no, if they know that you also try to be fair.

Sometimes, of course, the answer is simply No, without a silver lining attached. "Can I make a bottle rocket?" will never be answered with "Not now, but perhaps after dinner." Some things are not negotiable, and kids need—and deserve— straight answers.

What about times when you can't be fair? Whenever my kids come whining to me that "it's not fair," I put my arm around their shoulders and remind them that this is an excellent lesson in what life is really like. Life is not fair, I tell them. But then I remind them that sometimes, the pendulum also swings tremendously in their favor. And they should expect to see both strokes of luck throughout their lives. Then I carefully point out those moments of great fortune, and I remind them that these times will balance out the days when things seem unfair.

Set the limits for your family, and do not waffle! First, you and your husband need to agree to back one another up. Show your kids that there will be no playing one against the other. Our kids know that if we discover they've asked Mom when Dad has already said no—or vice versa—there will be very unpleasant consequences.

You might have a family council, where you let the kids help make the rules and establish the consequences for breaking them. This works amazingly well. In fact, kids often attach a harsher punishment to infractions than you would, and you might have to soften their initial suggestions. Don't be a family suffocating in a sea of picky rules. Be clear on the big stuff, and ease off on the tiny stuff. Remember, you live in a house of people, not a House of Representatives. You dilute the power of the important "laws" by cluttering up the books with zillions of petty ones.

Establish a no-whining policy. NEVER give in to a request if it was whined for, *even if you were going to do it anyway.* Change your plan and drive home the point that WHINING MEANS YOU WON'T GET IT.

Don't get sucked into the consumerism that seems to be consuming families these days. Just before Brandon celebrated his eleventh birthday, I asked him if he wanted anything in particular. "Well, I don't really know," he said. "I haven't been watching that much TV, so I haven't seen the commercials."

Can you believe this?!?!

Well, I told myself, at least we're doing TV right. Now we have to teach this kid that you don't let advertisers dictate what you want, and blur that line between wants and needs. Kids also need to understand that the toys their friends have are not necessarily going to be duplicated under *your* Christmas tree. Don't let children define their personal satisfaction by whether they have the right label clothing, the latest rollerblades, or the fanciest computer.

And if you happen to have more money than you need, send it to me. No, seriously, if you happen to be wealthy, still make kids wait. Help them earn the toy. Teach them that immediate gratification is what babies scream for, not what people do who are trying to grow up and mature. Let them learn to appreciate, instead of expect.

I think this is a good time to bring out the role models. Go to the library and get books on great people, even "cool" people your kids will like to learn about, who made it and found joy and success—and who never had a Nintendo. Teach them that success is not tied to money or things. Show them people in situations very much like your child's who really did something exciting with their lives. Point out that these people developed *discipline*.

You also teach discipline by being disciplined yourself. As with everything, example is the best teacher. Look at your life and see where you might improve in showing your children the benefits of discipline. Toot your own horn—tell them how you dislike mowing the lawn, but you do it because it has to be done. (They may have thought you enjoyed it all this time!) Teach them that sometimes we must do difficult things, and we have to simply persevere through them to accomplish what we want to.

"My mommy likes to iron," said a little boy in a school I once visited. "She does it all the time."

I smiled and doubted that the mother really enjoyed ironing, but simply because she had to do it so often, the boy *assumed* she must be doing what she enjoyed. Let kids know when you are using discipline to accomplish a task!

We all have to learn to sacrifice and make adjustments to live fully and have ultimate happiness. Life isn't truly fulfilling if we take the easy road, party all the time, or act like carefree children forever. People who behave this way do not succeed, and do not benefit the world or those around them. They make poor marriages, do not last at jobs, and drift along blindly in a self-centered world. They never grow past the adolescent, hedonistic phase. (You may even have dated a couple of people like this!)

But you want more than that for your children. So you must teach—and model—discipline. Stick to your word, and let kids feel strength in what you say. If your kids are always arguing with you and trying to get you to change your stance, you have probably allowed them to win at this game before.

You can change. Simply stop caving in. You are the parent! Believe in yourself! Your kids need a strong mom, not one who is afraid of her own kids. You can give them reasons; that's fine. But telling them why is not an invitation to debate; it's simply a gift you're providing as a freebie. The answer should still be firm.

CHAPTER 23

The Disappearing Room Mom

I've gotta admit, I love this one. It plugs the hole of being unable to say no, then finding yourself spread so thin that you can't possibly be an effective mother.

Are you like me? Do you say "yes" to bring fruit salad to the school party on the same day that you're starting your period, having a root canal, and expecting house guests? What are we—nuts? Are we gluttons for stress?

If we knew in our hearts that we were good mothers, we wouldn't feel one pinch of guilt for saying no to the fruit salad assignment.

Well, I am no longer like that, and you needn't be, either.

I can't say that there's a magic trick to changing. I simply woke up one day and, like people who have suddenly quit smoking, I quit knocking myself out. I realized that saying no to someone *outside* my family usually meant being able to say yes to someone *inside* my family. It just struck me as a great idea.

I still volunteer. In fact, I still serve on the symphony board, and once a week I teach mothering skills to inner-city moms. I volunteer at my church. I also go along on occasional school field trips and help with the school chess club every Monday. I've agreed to be room mom once for each child. But

I've drawn sharp limits. I still say no far more than I say yes. I weigh each request before I give an answer, and I'll do it only if I am absolutely certain it's something I *want* to do. Most of the service I render at the schools is visible to my children. I still have two pre-schoolers who need me, and they come before outside requests.

Pick your priorities and chuck the rest, gals. Don't just crawl under a blanket and refuse to do *anything*. But cut down if you have over-extended. Take a close look at the reasons why you feel compelled to get involved in certain things. Is it so you'll be seen by the right people? Is it for status, or to belong to a certain group? Is it so you'll be perceived as busy or generous? Is it because somebody else is doing it? Is it because you like to run things? Unless your motives are altruistic, think hard before saying yes. That's actually the standard I use when someone calls and makes a request of me: Do I want to do this for my family, or just so I will appear a certain way to others? It's a great standard for measuring.

I also pick the kinds of activities that are down my alley— things that fit my personality. I would never, for example, volunteer to keep the books for the PTA. In such a scenario, I can see myself handcuffed and dragged away for embezzling funds that I never knew existed. While I think of myself as personally frugal, bookkeeping is at the bottom of my talent stack.

So I know my limits and I serve in ways that appeal to me personally. I love working with the inner-city moms and teaching them parenting skills. It's not an assignment that I took on with a sigh of reluctance; it's something I can't wait to do each week.

I also like to cook, so I can usually be counted on to bring food when needed. If you are not a cook, for heaven's sake, don't agree to help! Bring the paper plates and cups. Or help with publicity.

Sometimes I help students with their writing. This kind of

volunteering fits me like a glove. Years ago, I produced and hosted my own daily TV talk show in Los Angeles; so to volunteer to set up lectures and panelists for the parent education arm of the school is something that feels like second nature to me. Not only that, but because I know how to do it, it's a lot easier for me than it would be for someone else, who might have cringed at such an assignment.

I know a mother who's a fantastic fund raiser. She has more connections than AT&T. And you have never met a more charming saleswoman. She can talk donations and gifts out of anybody. Put this gal in charge of your activity, and she'll have free airline tickets within the hour. She's the one to do that.

Me? Forget it. My sales pitch goes something like, "Hi, I know I'm probably catching you at a bad time, and you can say no at any point, so please don't feel you have to do this, but you wouldn't want to donate a dollar to the candy drive, would you?" Any top salesman could read that pitch and find ten major mistakes I'd made even before taking my first breath. I am definitely not the person you want as a fund raiser.

So know your strengths and weaknesses, and if you do agree to volunteer, do it in ways that you enjoy, and in ways that are your forte.

Whatever you do, be careful that you don't let the things which matter least take precedence over the things which matter most. Otherwise, guilt will be a monkey on your back that you'll never shake off.

Some time ago, my three best friends and I were talking about how easily our time gets gobbled up if we're not careful. I was feeling pretty disgusted with all the junk that had crowded into my life, and I said, "You know what I'm going to do the next time someone asks me to do something? Laugh and hang up." Somehow my bold suggestion got us laughing, and we joked that "Laugh and Hang Up" would make a great

T-shirt slogan for oppressed mothers everywhere. Of course, I can't be as rude as that, but I can certainly stick to my plan to pare down and give my best time to my best buddies: the members of my own family.

CHAPTER 24

Speaking Your Kids' Language

I have never met a married couple who never disagreed. Oh, sure, I've heard couples *claim* that this is so. But I usually scoff and toss that fabrication right out like a promise to lower taxes.

I simply do not believe that any two people are so perfectly alike, so utterly compatible, that they have never had one disagreement. Even identical twins have disagreements, and it's a cinch that you and your husband are much less alike than identical twins! (Remember, Wrigley said that in a corporation, whenever two men always agree, one of them is unnecessary!)

Most people expect to be different—not incompatible, but certainly different from one another. And yet, one of the biggest areas of difference is one that most people never realize during their whole married life.

The two of you probably speak different languages.

Huh?

Yep.

Sure, you both speak English. But I'm talking about the language of love. Unless your husband was raised in your same home, he grew up with different parents who expressed their love in other ways than your parents did. Maybe his folks were the quiet type, showing their love with trim lawns and fresh sheets. Maybe their family ran on the monetary system, where people knew they were loved if things were bought for them. Or maybe his was a physically affectionate family, for whom hugs and kisses were the expression of love. Perhaps his family talked to show love, praising accomplishments and explaining their feelings verbally. Maybe they even showed caring by criticizing and correcting one another.

Regardless, it's a cinch that you and your husband will stumble, if you haven't already, over missed cues. You'll bake him a cake to let him know how proud you are of his raise, and he'll feel hurt that you didn't *say* more. Or he'll take you on a vacation to boost your spirits, and you'll still long for a night of wild passion instead.

We all need to teach our husbands our own language. And they need to teach us theirs! Don't be afraid to let your husband know what it is you're waiting for. He cannot read your mind any better than you can read his.

Sit down and talk it over. Maybe you're highly verbal, but all your words just roll off him as he waits for a hug. Maybe he does every repair job in the house to show you how much he loves you, but you're waiting for an intimate chat.

If you don't speak the same language, don't worry—few couples match perfectly, even if they're both the same "type." Just learn the other one's language, and show love in the way your husband can best understand it! That's what compromise in a marriage is all about.

It's exactly the same with children.

I believe that God has a sense of humor. Or maybe he just knows we need to stretch and grow in areas we wouldn't have chosen. But, at least in my case, he has given me a mixed bag of four children whose personalities couldn't be more disparate. Each one requires an entirely different parental approach, and usually at the exact same moment.

I see families where all the kids are type B easygoing

pleasers, and I sigh. Why couldn't mine all be alike? Or I'll see families where every kid is an overachiever—or an under-achiever—or a show-off—or shy—and the same tricks work the same way on all their kids.

Then there are my kids, who appear to be completely unre-lated to each other. It's a juggling act, like spinning plates on long sticks—only I have a plate, a banana, a bowling pin, and a porcupine to keep spinning.

Maybe you've noticed the same thing. Maybe you have a defiant child who couldn't care less if he upsets you, and a sen-sitive child who dissolves into tears if you even glance in her direction.

YOU NEED TO LEARN A DIFFERENT LANGUAGE FOR EVERY PERSON YOU TRULY CARE ABOUT.

Otherwise, you're expecting everybody else to learn *your* language and accept love the way *you're* willing to dole it out, in brittle refusal to accommodate anyone but yourself. Not exactly the way to win family and influence children.

"I'm not a talker. I'll show them I care by all the things I do," one mother said. But what if words are what one of her kids desperately needs? How can a mother who's refusing to try, ever reduce her guilt? If you try to learn the languages of those you love, you'll automatically reduce guilt, because you'll be a better mother, *and you'll know it.*

We all know that we have different learning styles. Some kids are visual learners and grasp concepts best by reading them on a written page. Other kids learn physically and need to feel tangible, textured letters to learn their alphabet, or jump and climb on a giant sculptured letter. Still others are auditory learners and learn best by listening, without the dis-traction of having to look, read, or feel. And so it goes.

It's the same with communicating love. There's a certain language for every child. They even have separate body lan-guages! To miss physical cues is to miss important opportunities to show love and caring. If you notice a person's posture, and you try to address a hurt, let's say, that person will know that you care. You noticed the way their body *looked,* without having to be hit over the head. You picked up on a subtlety. This alone communicates genuine concern.

And you teach your children, by example, to be equally sensitive to others. They will make better mates and parents themselves because you taught them to notice the way other people are behaving.

The kids were in the car with me the other day, playing an Elvis tape to tease me (it is safe to assume that I am not an Elvis Presley fan). "I just want you kids to know," I said, "that if I weren't driving right now, my body language would be folded arms."

"Mine is a grin," Brandon said, craning his neck into the front seat like Ernest smiling into a fish-eye lens, and making sure I could see every tooth in his head. Naturally, at that point each child had to join the celebration, trying to top the last one with more and more exaggerated postures of glee.

I've even coaxed hurt feelings from a reluctant pouter by saying, "Okay, don't *tell* me what's wrong. Just show me. Sit down and put your hands and legs how you think you're feeling right now." Invariably, as I try to guess what they're depicting, they do end up talking and explaining their feelings to me.

We talked about goals in an earlier chapter, and I thought I'd share a few of mine that had to do with language specifically.

A few months after Cassidy was born, I was poking through our closets for some of the baby toys my older sons had used. Most of their toys had been bent, lost, dismembered or eaten, but the survivors had found their way into storage, and deserve to be studied by NASA or somebody, to determine which substances are the most indestructible on earth.

One of the boxes I stumbled upon, quite literally, in a darkened attic, turned out to contain some of my own memorabilia from high school days ("The Olden Days" according to my sons, who think life without a VCR is life in the Mesozoic Era). I had written on the front of an envelope in decisive, confident lettering, "My Goals."

Inside, I had listed every conceivable wish my teenage mind could imagine, under the topics Intellectual, Physical, Emotional, Social, Financial, Spiritual, and Family. It was as if writing it down could make my wishes come true, and I had left no stone unturned. I smiled as I read some of the goals I had reached (earn a master's degree, have several children, travel around the world, stay out of debt), and ached inside as I saw others I hadn't achieved.

Some of the goals I missed were contingent upon age. I thought I'd be able to sell five books by the time I was 30. Wrong. Only one of them had sold by that magic date. I also wanted to learn French, German, and Spanish by that age. (The word "quadralingual" held great appeal in those days.) Wrong again. The most I can claim in the linguistics department is enough Spanish to get by, and that's only because most Latinos are extremely patient and willing to play charades with me.

I tucked the envelope into the pocket of a shirt which my goal sheet said I should have personally designed—but which I bought on sale last year—and finished hunting for baby toys.

Through the day, I kept thinking about some of my missed targets, and not learning another language kept coming back to haunt me. Maybe I should have taken night classes after the kids were in bed. Maybe I could still learn three languages after the kids were grown and gone. Maybe the goal was unrealistic in the first place—a goal at odds with parenthood, like going off on an archeology dig for ten months, or putting expensive modern sculptures on low tables.

That afternoon, Brandon—who had recently announced

that his name was now Spike— was surrounded by his action toy figures, and was wearing green water paint on his face for camouflage. He invited me to play army with him.

Last time we had done this, I had arranged the little men in a chorus line and had them all kicking together and singing, "Oh, we're the Army dancers, the Army dancers—" at which point Brandon—pardon me, Spike—had abruptly dismissed me from the game, rolling his eyes and shaking his head.

This was my second chance, and I didn't want to blow it. "Okay, you think you're so tough," I snarled in behalf of one plastic army man to another, "Let's see you catch this grenade!" Brandon's eyes danced with joy and he immediately answered for my opponent, "Oh, yeah? Well, I have a magic shield. So there!"

"Rats," I said, helping my little man to slink away. "I'm foiled again." Brandon beamed.

Soon Richie, who had been playing at a neighbor's, came home in tears over not being allowed to use their bike jump. He ran to his room and closed the door. Last time something hurt his feelings, I had given him some time to be alone and collect his thoughts. Richie had felt utterly abandoned.

This time I went right to him, held him, and let him talk about the situation. By the end of our chat, Richie understood what had actually happened (he was too young), and even admitted that the bike jump had looked a little scary.

"What?!" I said, pretending to be mad and tickling him. "You mean you tricked me? You told me you wanted to go on that jump, and now I find out you didn't even want to? And I'm sitting here wiping your tears and jumping up and down? (and then, of course, I jumped up and down) And it was all for *nothing*?"

Richie was dissolved in giggles on the floor, thrilled at the idea of pulling a fast one on Mommy. Though it really hadn't been a joke, Richie was happy again, probably just knowing that I cared enough to take time for him.

That night as I put Cassidy to bed, we played peek-a-boo. He seemed to like it best when I turned my head away, and then snapped it back to look at him, rather than the way the older two boys had played it, where I'd cover my face with my hands and then open them up.

And suddenly it hit me: I hadn't missed that goal, after all. I *was* speaking three other languages. I was tailoring my parenting to each boy, using the words and the style he most understood. Brandon spoke Armyan, a difficult language for me, but one which I have finally mastered. And Richie spoke Sensi-tease, a complex tongue which must be spoken carefully, as the possibility of offending native speakers is very high. Little Cassidy spoke Gamish, smiling most broadly when games were played *his* way, instead of the standard way.

With every child you have to learn a new language, a new set of rules so special, so individual, that there are no classes available for instruction, and no manuals on the subject. It's a goal I never would have thought to write down as a teenager. Who would have thought its fulfillment could become one of my most crowning achievements?

SECTION FIVE

Putting Guilt On a Diet

CHAPTER 25

Blow Your Own Horn!

Motherhood is no place for modesty. Acting demure, graciously accepting praise, and denying how wonderful you are, are all things you do at a banquet of career professionals. With kids, you've got to blow your own horn.

Children do not come to us as natural thankers. They do not spring into appreciative, grateful beings without some instruction. From the time my children were babies, I'd tell them to "say thank you" as I handed them things. At first, babies must be startled. After all, doesn't the whole world revolve around them and exist to make them happy? Kids just don't get it, and *won't* get it unless you're willing to teach gratitude.

And so we train them. We make them write thank-you notes. We send them back to their friends' front doors to thank the hostess of the birthday party. We tell them to thank people who compliment them. Otherwise, they'd have no clue.

And this training is a good thing. But in teaching them to be civilized folks who appreciate kindnesses, we mustn't stop short of teaching them to appreciate their mothers! You've heard of music appreciation class? How about parent appreciation?

If you don't insist that your kids appreciate all that you do for them, you'll wind up with teenagers who feel entitled. They'll *expect* you to wash their gym socks, drive them to ball games, take them shopping, and let them have the car whenever the fancy strikes them. They'll be spoiled, demanding, and ultimately, miserable.

Does this mean we whine and complain, listing every sacrifice and chore we've done on their behalf today? That would shovel heaps of guilt onto our children, and leave the grownups depressed as well! Instead, we should share our efforts joyfully, as matters of fact.

Let kids know how much you enjoy what you do for them. "I love the hours I spend taking you to piano lessons because I can see so much progress." "I'm so glad I was able to postpone my appointment so I could come to the game. This is terrific." If your time is given with resentment, it's not a gift anyone would want. But kids do need to know that adults have lives too, and that we are sacrificing something else in order to put them first.

Bob and I also let our children know that when a sacrifice has been made for them, we expect responsibility on their part. If we're spending X dollars a month to rent the trombone our eldest boy asked to play, then it's his job to practice it. If he doesn't, the trombone will (and did) go back. Now *he* has to earn the rental money.

One evening at dinner, my husband suddenly turned to the children and said, "Do you kids have any idea what your mother did for you today?" He then went on to list the supplies I had purchased for a school project, the other errands I had run, the volunteering at two of our kids' schools, the laundry and cleaning, the cooking, the orthodontist appointments made, etc., etc. You know the routine—it's *your* routine, too! And it's even more overwhelming for moms who work outside the home. I keep a daytimer filled with things I need to do, and I cannot fathom how any mother makes it through her day without one.

The children's eyes grew round as they listened (and I began feeling even more exhausted as I realized what I had crammed into that day!), but I could see appreciation taking place. Kids need to be caught by the sleeve sometimes and reminded of just how much is being done for them while they're off playing or in a classroom.

And it's okay to coach them and say, "Repeat after me: Thank you, Mother." Do it with humor. Throw in a dramatic flourish—why not? It may seem contrived at first, but believe me, you are teaching positive habits, and eventually kids will realize that expressing appreciation is not only the right thing to do, but it feels good to both speaker and recipient. Courtesy builds respect and love.

This doesn't mean our children bow and scrape to us (ha!), or that we make them feel unworthy of all we do for them. In fact, as I was driving the children home the other day, they suddenly began discussing what belongings they wanted when Bob and I kick the bucket. "I want the grandfather clock," one of them announced. "I get that antique thing with the mirror on it," another one piped up. On and on they went.

"Hey," I said, "stop grabbing up all our stuff! We're not even dead yet!"

Richie shrugged. "Well, why wait 'til the last minute?"

Apparently, every kid is a comedian. See, even if you *try* to teach them to earn things, and to value what they have, they'll still "expect" to come out on the receiving end. A lot of that just goes with youth. All the more reason to be vigilant in your insistence that they appreciate you and what you do.

When Bob and I first married, he was stunned at how often I said "Really?" when he complimented me on something. He thought I was questioning his honesty. What I was actually doing, and did not hesitate to explain, was milking the moment for some extra praise. Sometimes I just need a little more syrup on my waffles, you know? If he said, "I like how you've arranged the pictures," my "Really?" meant "Go on." I was ready for him to really lay it on thick.

One day I had cut several flowers from our yard and arranged them in a large bouquet on the dining table. Bob saw them but didn't say anything. Naturally, I went fishing for compliments. "So, how do you like the flower arrangement?" I asked.

"Nice," Bob said.

Ha ha ha. As if he could get by with a one-word response.

"Come see it from all sides," I said, dragging him into the dining room to circle my creation. Well, by now, Bob got the picture, and began going overboard, raving about my flower arrangement until even I became saturated and had to stop him. To this day, if I say, "How do you like this?" or "How does this look?" Bob gives me a glance and says, "Is this another flower arrangement?" If so, he knows he needs to exaggerate a bit.

And my kids have not escaped the flower arrangement syndrome, either. If I've worked hard on something for a child and he passes it off with a shrug, I grab him by the arm, swing him into a hug and say, "Excuse me, did you just tell me how lucky you are to have such a wonderful mother?"

"Uh, yeah," the child usually says, a sheepish grin on his face.

"I thought so," I say, releasing him.

Do not wash, dry, iron, fold, and deliver clean laundry to your children without some acknowledgment! This is not something they should expect and take for granted. This is a loving thing you have done as their mother, and at the very least, they need to say, "Thanks, Mom." Believe me, you will feel greater self-esteem and less guilt when you demand respect.

And I am not the only person who gets applauded; I see that the children compliment their father and one another, too. These are not shallow bits of lip service; they are appropriate expressions of appreciation for real favors.

Okay, perhaps I do go overboard raving to my children about how marvelous they are. But it's not with ulterior motives to inspire behavior that actually doesn't exist, or to lavish praise upon a child I have been over-criticizing. When I'm gaga over something they've done, it's sincere.

A scene comes to mind, when Brandon had constructed an elaborate city of blocks and action figures. I came upon his room—which to the casual observer looked like a shambles—and went on and on about how cleverly he had designed a tunnel, how ingeniously he had planned the airport and harbor, how symmetrically he had built a castle. Finally, Brandon said, "C'mon, Mom, it's not *that* great." Well, to me it was.

Once at a piano competition for Richie, he played a piece I had heard him practice at home a hundred times, but this time it sounded like an angel was playing. The notes resonated like never before! It brought me to tears, and with a choked-up voice I proudly told him that I had never heard him play that piece so beautifully. I still remember Richie chuckling and saying, "Mom." Then he lowered his voice. "That's because our piano at home doesn't have a pedal." Oh.

Well, okay. So perhaps my boys don't need quite the level of enthusiasm that occasionally spills forth. But they don't wonder if they're appreciated. And you shouldn't wonder if you are appreciated as a mother, either. If your family isn't coming up with the thanks on their own, by golly, it's all right to teach them how!

Not only will your family learn the fine art of appreciation, but *you* will gain new confidence in your abilities as well. Just watch your guilt level shrink as you command respect and acknowledgment. And, by pointing out your positive efforts to others, you'll be forced to confront them yourself. You'll realize that you're actually doing a pretty good job!

Even if you must say so yourself. And, sometimes, you simply must.

CHAPTER 26

Accentuate the Positive

I just taught you how to get others to notice your best efforts. But let's be realistic: It's usually tougher for most of us to see those highlights in ourselves.

To truly put guilt on a diet, you need to keep a running list of things you did right. We all make mistakes, and I'm not saying we should ignore them. But guilty mothers tend to dwell on one error, and completely overlook the ten great things they *did* do.

So you need a notebook and a pencil. Every time you "do it right," or feel a twinge of success, write it down. Your perspective will change, and you'll begin looking for these little "peak moments" of performance. I guarantee that within a few days of beginning such a log, you'll be amazed at how many entries you can actually write!

Is this a brag sheet? You betcha. Why not? Motherhood should be fun, right? It's your main job, isn't it? Would an arctic explorer not keep a journal of the great things he discovered along his journey? Would a pioneer not catalog the hardships he endured and the triumph of his achievements? It doesn't mean these people are boasting. They're just sharing their joy in a job well done.

And you, my dear, have the toughest job on this planet.

When something goes right, you can give yourself a little parade, right there on paper. Catalog all your successes, all the times motherhood was the joy you knew it would be. Note all the days when you know you earned an A.

I'll share a few of mine, so you'll see what I mean.

Entry #1: "As the mother of four extremely active children (one has attention deficit disorder, and does not hold still for anything), I sometimes fall into bed at night, exhausted from simply holding the line all day. At times, I've wondered if my rough-and-tumble kids are missing the tender side of life (guilt, again!).

"But one morning my then six-year-old son woke me up by climbing into bed with me and whispering, 'I love your face so much I feel all tickly. You are the goodest mommy in the whole world. Can I smell your lipstick? You are a rainbow swan. Will your cheeks always be so soft? I love you so much, I could just squeeze your whole, skinny hand off. When I grow up and marry you, I'm going to give you a whole list of cars.'

"I laughed and gave my little guy a squeeze. Suddenly, I had not only enough energy to meet the new day, but a tickly feeling of my own inside, telling me that this one morning had made all the others well worth it."

Entry #2: "Every Wednesday the school lets children buy ice cream at lunchtime. Brandon [then age five], who loves ice cream with a chocolate passion, had lost his quarter and was heartsick. Across the room, a little girl—also missing her quarter—was on the verge of tears.

"Soon everyone else raced outside for their treats. Brandon shuffled out slowly, his hands in his pockets, his gaze to the ground. Suddenly, he caught a glimpse of something shiny on the playground. A quarter! He dashed over and picked it up, elated.

"Then he glanced back toward the classroom, where the little girl was still crying. He walked back in and gave her the brand new quarter. Her face lit up and she thanked him, dashing outside to join the ice cream line.

"'I saw the whole thing and just had to call and tell you,' his kindergarten teacher said. 'It was the most loving gesture I've ever seen. I hope you don't mind, but I would like to buy Brandon an ice cream—my treat.'

"One of the toughest traits to teach a child is compassion, but this day was my treat: The efforts of motherhood had paid off."

Entry #3: "While my two young sons played nearby, I rolled up my sleeves and began to dig. The garden was badly overgrown, and much as I detest gardening, I knew the work had to be done. That morning I had bought perhaps too many plants at the nursery, and I had to work quickly to get them all into the ground.

"An hour later, after digging an especially large hole, breaking through roots and chiseling out rocks, I heard a small pattering noise behind me. When I turned, there was my then five-year-old, perched on a rock, applauding.

"'Do you know why I'm clapping?' he said. 'Because you dug that hole so well!'

"I laughed and gave him a big hug. Of all the work I've done in my life, I have never received a standing (well, a perching) ovation. This singular, precious moment stands out to me as proof that motherhood is not a thankless job. Its smallest tasks are appreciated by those who matter most of all—our children."

Entry #4: This one happened when Richie was about six. "Richie and I were sitting on the front porch, just having a lazy afternoon together, and he looked up at me and said, 'On the last day of my being playful, I want to play with you the whole day. I sure hope it's on a Saturday.'"

Entry #5: "We all try to raise honest children who'll make the right choices when they come to crossroads in their lives.

But we never know if we've succeeded until our child finds himself in a tempting situation where his integrity's really on the line—will he cave in or stand strong?

"My then nine-year-old, Richie, recently faced such a choice. At recess, his classmates had been playing basketball, and time was nearly up. Richie's team was behind by one, and an opponent threw a pass that grazed Richie's arm before going out of bounds.

"'Don't tell them it touched you,' one boy hissed, 'then we can get the ball and make a basket.'

"No one else knew whether the ball had actually touched Richie or not. But Richie raised his hand. 'It touched me last,' he said. The ball went to the other team, who threw it in and won the game.

"'Why did you tell?' Richie's teammates marched angrily off the court. 'Nobody would have known!'

"Richie faced them squarely. 'I'm not a boy who lies,' he said, 'and I would have known.'

"For me, that's a mother's payment. That's what it really means to win the game."

There are less dramatic entries that still make me smile, if only because I can see our children's senses of humor developing. One night when Bob and I had left for a date together, we reminded the children not to touch the video recorder. Richie left us this note taped to the door when we got home: "I was really good while you were gone. I even have proof of it on videotape."

Occasionally when I re-read these kinds of entries in my motherhood journal, I wonder how can I ever doubt my worth, or doubt whether I'm doing a good enough job. And as I wipe away the tears, I recall what Richie once said: "Sometimes you just get so full of feelings, you can't hold them anymore and they leak out your eyes."

We all have days when we want to crow—about our chil-

dren, or even about ourselves. Days when we held our tempers. Days when we laughed with our kids, went kite-flying, dried a tear and taught an important lesson, delivered a basket of goodies to a neighbor together—life is filled with positive moments worth writing down. Do it! Don't let another day slip by, when you didn't keep a record of the little successes. And then re-read them from time to time. Especially on days when you feel an extra load of guilt. Read the up side. Get your footing back and boost your confidence.

This is not head-in-the-sand optimism. If you'd feel better about it, make a giant list of all your failings and mistakes, have a good cry, forgive yourself, and tear up the list. Get rid of it with a neat, clean ending. *Then* go on to catalog the joys and successes.

You could make just as thick a journal if you look for the goofs, as if you look for the triumphs. But which one will really do you more good? Which one will your children save forever and ever, as the legacy you will someday leave them?

Call it a book of blessings, if you like—days when you lucked out and everything magically went right. Don't even claim credit if you don't feel comfortable doing so. It will still reduce guilt if you focus on the good things.

When the end of the day comes, and Mom collapses into a chair where the children left a puddle of glue and a popsicle three hours ago, she can still smile. She can use humor, determination, and a believe-in-yourself attitude to remind her that she is doing just great. And as she counts her blessings, she'll even include the two little blessings who got to that chair.

CHAPTER 27

The Working Woman's
Bag of Tricks

Hey, hey. I know that stay-at-home moms are also "working women." There is not, to my knowledge, a kind of adult woman who does *not* work. If there are hours in a day, we'll work 'em. It doesn't matter if we're running an office or a washing machine—we all work 'til we drop.

In fact, I'd like to propose an end to this battle between the outside-career moms and the stay-at-home moms. We can do so much to benefit children if we *combine* our efforts, instead of dividing and competing. There's a sisterhood here that we all share—a common goal of raising great children, of improving society, of feeling fulfilled, of having happy relationships.

You know what caused that little domestic battle, don't you? It's guilt. If we really believed that we were great moms, we'd have no need to be defensive. Nobody could topple our confidence. No stay-at-home mother would blush when someone asked her, "What do you do?" at a dinner party. "I'm a mom," she'd say, brimming with enthusiasm, not needing to remind anyone of her master's degree or her career before staying home. If anybody wrinkled their noses, she'd breeze right by them. That's *their* problem, she'd think.

And without guilt, working women wouldn't feel defensive, either. They wouldn't explain how they juggle career and children, they wouldn't quote experts who defend their choice, or scoff at women who've chosen another path. They'd just calmly do their job and do their mothering and feel good about the whole of it.

Ah, if only it were so simple. But that's actually the kind of confidence I want you to have. Stop wringing your hands because you work or you don't work! If you *want* to stay home, and that's an option, for heaven's sake give your two weeks' notice. Stop being untrue to yourself. Is there a way you can stay home while the children are young, then re-enter the workplace later? Likewise, if you feel you need to work, follow that inspiration, and don't let busybody advice cloud your judgment.

And yet, for mothers who do work outside the home, there seems to be an extra measure of guilt to overcome. Perhaps it's justified in some cases. What are your reasons for working? If they're strictly selfish, count on guilt as a constant companion. But if your motives are more noble than simply affording a bigger house, stop beating yourself.

Many working mothers feel guilty because they're away from the house, they can't go along on field trips, or bake cookies for the Valentine party. They see other moms apparently "doing more." Again, resist the urge to compare. Everyone approaches motherhood differently. Perhaps other moms are seeing all that you provide *your* child and envying *you!*

For the wonderful working mothers who are doing their best to rear their children, I have compiled a list of a dozen ways they can put their guilt on a diet:

First, particularly if you can't always talk to your children when you're working, set aside some "You and Me" time once you're home. Turn off the TV! Unwind after the kids are in bed. Give them some focused attention when you *are* home.

Second, plan mini-trips. Vacation time doesn't have to be lazy time. Remember, there are fifty-two weekends a year. Kids whose parents cannot lounge around with them all summer need not be deprived of family vacation experiences. You can duplicate all the same memories and excursions in two days every so often, as you can in seven days straight.

Third, take time for your marriage. Just because you're working doesn't mean you have to ignore your marriage and give every available minute to the children. They need to remember that this is the Number One relationship in the house. Of course, you want one-on-one time with the kids as well, but keep your marriage in good working order.

Fourth, become an activist for at-work support for sick-child care and modified work schedules. Your employer wants you there, and wants to keep you happy with your company.

Fifth, get creative and see how flexible you can make your work situation. Design your own job! Is there a portion of your work that can be done at home? Could you agree to work extra hours one week to get fluctuating hours the next? Can you share your schedule with another busy parent? Are there related fields, with more flexible formats, that you could transition into?

Along with this idea, choose one field trip to attend each year. Or one school play. Surely you have *some* vacation or personal time off each year. You can even use it for doctor's visits, if you feel guilty about someone else taking your child to these appointments. I mentioned that I agreed to be room mom for each of my children *once*. Sometimes a job like that is a matter of phone calling; even a career mother can find some evening time to do that.

Sixth, don't suffocate your child when you are together, trying to make up for being away. No Hovercrafts in the living room! This sounds like a rule for kids, but it's meant for *you.* We often think stay-at-home moms are most at risk for crowding or pushing their children, but career moms are offenders, too. They sometimes hover because they've missed out all day. They try to force intimacy and sharing, instead of letting it click naturally. Be available, but don't smother your children.

Seventh, give yourself some slack. One mom I know jokes that if she has less time with her kids, there's less room for error! Don't be a perfectionist. Be realistic. Know that even stay-at-home moms are not baking cookies and playing ring-around-the-rosy all day, focusing every second on the children. There's work to be done at home, too. No kid has a mother staring him in the face all day—and if he does, that kind of hovering can do more harm than good.

Eighth, call every day to check in with your child, right after the child gets home from school. Make that connection one she can count on. You need it, too.

Ninth, make your talks count. Don't always get into a heavy discussion (kids will see you coming and take off in the other direction!), but use the time you do have to get close. Ask probing questions, questions that teach, questions that make your child think.

Tenth, create a stimulating environment for your child. Even leave her a surprise or a note to find when she gets home from school. Fill your house with the best books, and limit TV and computer game time. You don't have to physically be there to enforce obedience; rules can and should exist even when you are not there.

Eleventh, play and laugh together. Share the fun of childhood before it slips into adulthood. Share hobbies, riddles and games.

Twelfth, even when you must be away, remind your child that you have her best interests at heart *always,* and that your favorite time is time with her.

CHAPTER 28

Perfectionism Poison

To really put guilt on a diet, eliminate perfectionism. Think logically about it: If you continually hold yourself up to an impossibly high ideal, you'll always fall short, you'll feel like a failure, and thus you will become a guilt junkie.

Perfectionism not only ruins your own happiness, but it's contagious. You'll raise other little perfectionists who'll be as guilt-ridden as you are. They'll never enjoy their efforts, because their efforts will never be quite good enough. What a sad way to waste a lifetime.

Anyone who wishes to learn this lesson has only to take a vacation with her family. Nothing insures disaster more quickly than the act of traveling somewhere and expecting things to go smoothly.

We don't actually plan the problems, but Travel Trouble has nevertheless become a cherished tradition (cherished in retrospect, usually) in our household. Maybe yours is the same way.

It's almost a sacrilege if we get a hundred miles from the house without some sort of disaster. There's the ceremonial breaking down of the car in a rural hamlet that is famous—at least to us—for never having the automotive part we need. Then there's the customary Loss of Reservations, followed by Loss of Composure in hotel lobbies across America. The

Joni Hilton

"Where's My Blankie?" ritual which involves toddler hysteria and the mobilization of all six family members to hunt down the singularly most essential belonging, without which the trip cannot proceed. We are also equipped with Ice Water Pool Locators, and can find the one hotel swimming pool in the state with a broken heater.

But there's more. We also have talents for getting robbed, camping in poison ivy, taking the slow scenic routes during thick fog, and arriving at tourist attractions simultaneously with busloads of children on field trips.

And the bigger the budget, the grander the fiasco. On a budget-busting trip to Hawaii, I hid the excursion to Hanauma Bay like a surprise dessert, bringing it out at the end for a wonderful finale, a memory our kids were sure to relish for years. Ever the perfectionistic planner, I just knew they'd love snorkeling in Hawaii's crystal blue water, looking at the beautiful fish and coral. Everybody cheered. (Rule #1: Don't oversell.)

Bob and I spared no expense hiring a taxi to take us there, where I noted that I hadn't seen such a crowd since the Superbowl. Not to be discouraged, we promptly rented every known piece of snorkeling equipment. "Here, kids, put on these masks," I said, "so you can see the fish as you snorkel."

"It's pulling my hair," whined one child.

"Mine has salt water in it, and it's stinging my eyes," a brother lamented (the same salt water, I might add, in which he was happily splashing at another beach this same morning).

"The water's too cold," the eldest boy shivered, dipping one foot into the waves.

"No it's not," I smiled. "You'll love this. Don't you want to see the fish?"

Our youngest son squinted at the water. "I can see them from here," he said.

"Can't we go back to the hotel?" another boy asked.

"Oh, cut it out," I snapped. "Put this gear on this minute.

168

Now have fun."

I glanced at Bob, whose pockets were empty and whose eyes had turned into little Xs. "Ah, yes, another successful plan," he smirked. "Would you like to know the price tag of this little adventure?"

Now I was furious and began tossing snorkels and masks at various family members, snarling at them to be good sports. (Rule #2: Never use the same line the dentist uses.)

Nobody was buying it. The whining was escalating into tears, and Bob was whistling and trying to pretend this was all a bad dream. One boy began whining that I missed a spot when I put sunscreen on him. Another one was crying that I slathered on too much.

Finally we left, defeated, dragging our little pouters with us. (Rule #3: You can drag a kid to water, but you can't make him have a good time.)

On a trip Bob and I took alone to France, we thought we'd cruise the canals of Burgundy on a beautiful old barge. Sounds great, right? Bob fell through the kitchen floor. I kid you not . . . he was videotaping the elegant interior, walked backward into the kitchen, and fell straight down the hatch to the boiler room. He cracked a wooden step as thick as a bat, knocked himself cold, then came to and swore the crew to secrecy so I wouldn't panic and make him get an x-ray. To this day, whenever we tell this story, listeners ask, "Did you get it on videotape?"

I have two girlfriends whose budgets are a travel agent's dream. They decided to take their families on a lavish trip to Spain one summer. Do you think the kids talk about the Rock of Gibraltar? The castles? The Moorish influence, for heaven's sake? No. They talk about how many times their dads got lost trying to navigate the narrow, winding streets (even losing a rearview mirror once), and how funny it was when a passing bird bombed one of the moms at an outdoor cafe. This same experience could be duplicated at home, driving down an alley in a convertible, for no cost whatsoever.

And when we took our kids on an expensive skiing trip, do you think they remembered the price of the lift tickets? No. They remembered their mother, me, looking for a Chinese restaurant, seeing a Tai Kwon Do studio and saying, "Hey, that looks like a good place." To this day they hoot over the thought of their mother wandering into a karate studio and ordering an egg roll.

So I finally learned that it isn't how much you spend on a trip, how perfectly you plan it, or how sure you are that they'll love the dolphin show. What makes a happy family memory is if you've left room for calamity. Somehow, those times when we fall terribly short of the goal act like bonding glue. They cement us together as we tell and retell the mishaps and blunders. What appear to be vacation busts become our greatest laughs and stories.

Boy scouts don't come home raving about the fascinating difference between a spruce and a juniper. They come home roaring over the soggy tent, the leaky canoe, the fishhook caught in someone's pants, the underwear hung out to dry that scared everybody spitless at two a.m.

You could take your kids to the Bahamas, or to the nearest sea shore. Either way, they're going to come home giggling about the swimsuit that went fwap! right in front of everybody. Memories aren't made of money; they're made of time spent together.

And it's exactly the same with day-to-day life in your own home. Kids won't have fond memories of you criticizing the way they crossed their t's on a school report. They'll remember your arm around their shoulder, the cookies you brought them when they stayed up late studying, the way you let them make the bed crooked, as long as they were doing their best.

One of my kids' favorite memories is the time I tried to

show them how to make a Christmas gingerbread house with graham crackers. I figured this was the perfect way to let kids get involved and create a quick, colorful cottage, dripping with white icing and dotted with bright candies. They watched as I demonstrated how to mix the cement-like frosting. They watched as I set out several bowls of various candy decorations. They watched as I opened up a package of graham crackers and formed the walls and roof of a little house.

And then they howled and laughed until they fell off their chairs when it collapsed.

Kids *LIKE* to see grownups foiled. That's why it's so funny to them when a grown-up pretends he can't find his hat (which is on his head) and he turns round and round getting more and more exasperated. Kids find imperfection uproariously appealing. In fact, every year one of our family's Christmas traditions is now that crazy little "gingerbread" house that collapses every time. If it ever stands properly, the kids will be disappointed.

Holidays seem to bring out the perfectionist in some of us, so we need to be especially careful as our expectations climb. I recall one Valentine's Day when I had carefully arranged the kitchen breakfast bar with construction paper, lace doilies, pressed flowers, stickers, ribbons, candies—everything the kids could want to make gorgeous Victorian valentines for their classmates. As my two eldest sons reluctantly sat gluing and sticking, I tried to drum up some enthusiasm. "Try threading the ribbon through the lace like this," I gushed. The kids acted like they were half asleep.

Bob observed for a few minutes, then asked if he could speak with me around the corner. "These are *boys*," he said to an oblivious perfection-driven mother. "This is just like when you set up a play kitchen sink in their bedroom and then got mad that they didn't want to play with it. Boys don't *like* all that lacy, frilly stuff."

171

I stood there, half devastated, half embarrassed, with embarrassment slipping into a strong lead. How could I have been so blind to their obvious cues that they were only humoring me? All they really wanted to do was stick some store-bought Nintendo valentines into a few envelopes and be done with it. Yet, because I had always dreamed of my children making *perfect* Valentines, I completely overlooked the point of the holiday.

Family Circle magazine once asked me to write an article about overdoing the holidays; it would be titled "I Went Crazy Last Christmas." What an easy assignment, I thought; I go crazy *every* Christmas! I had no trouble confessing that I was a HolidayHolic. I told of my phone call to the zoo to inquire about renting real reindeer, my compulsion to have all the wrapping paper match the Christmas tree's theme (that year I had two trees—a teddy bear Christmas tree and a peaches-and-cream tree, dripping with pearls and satin). I had even coordinated the Christmas card envelopes to match the postage stamps!

I overbaked until I felt as if I were being held hostage in a spice factory. I overshopped until my Visa card was zipping through those laser readers faster than Santa zips through all those chimneys. But I knew I had set a new perfectionism record when I was tying the turkey's legs together and actually worried about whether the bow was straight.

Do you know that the editors at *Family Circle* thought I had made the whole thing up? Nobody could be *that* crazy, they said. So they edited it down to be more believable for publication!

Bob is the one who helped me turn over a new pine needle. He explained to me that the boys weren't crazy about a Christmas tree so dripping with peach satin and pearls that nobody could touch it. I had to lighten up and remember that families having fun and doing projects together is far more important than imposing my standard of perfection upon them. (And you know what? Our hodge-podge, multi-color Christmas tree is actually much more gorgeous and meaningful than the "designer" job I started with.)

We need to shoot for high goals, yes. But we also need to allow generous space for growth and experimentation. Just as you cannot plan a foolproof vacation, you cannot plan a foolproof life. And anguishing over every imperfection will only raise your level of stress, not your level of productivity.

If you back off on the demands you make of yourself, your kids will learn that they, too, don't have to be absolutely perfect every second. What a relief! What a warm, welcoming feeling that will be. And your own level of guilt will virtually vanish.

CHAPTER 29

Why I Don't Feel Guilty Anymore

I believe in talking to hands-on experts, not theorists in ivory towers. If I wanted to know about working conditions in a factory, I wouldn't ask a labor relations professor about it; I'd ask the woman sitting on the assembly line day in and day out.

It's the same with parenting. You can gather a lot of information from psychiatrists, family counselors and educators (and much of it is excellent); but for the straight scoop, I talk to mothers themselves. These are the soldiers in the trenches who know from practical experience what works and what doesn't.

Sometimes you learn the most from the people who feel they've failed. Often the parents of successful kids can't quite pinpoint what gave their kids an edge. But the mom whose children have led miserable lives have thought deeply and often about where things went wrong, and they can give you a detailed list of the things they'd do differently.

After talking with dozens of mothers, I've discovered that not all of them feel guilty. Ten mothers who look back without regret have shared with me some of their reasons why.

Mother #1: "I really resisted the urge to criticize. My own mother was so hypercritical of me that I vowed I would *never* copy her example. I bit my tongue a million times, but I never gave my kids negative labels."

Mother #2: "I had a wild love affair with my husband. Our kids knew it, too. I always let them see us kissing and hugging. They never doubted that we were in love. Even in their teens when they acted all embarrassed, I knew it gave them security to know that Mom and Dad were in love. Today, they're loving with their own husbands and wives."

Mother #3: "No matter how busy I was, I always stopped what I was doing to *listen* when my kids wanted to talk. I never wanted them to have a memory of me putting them off. Today we're very close, and I think that's one reason why."

Mother #4: "I made dinnertime a really big deal. We always talked, sitting around the table. Our kids even passed up being on some sports teams if it meant missing our dinner hour. It was just something important to our family, and the kids felt a strong sense of belonging."

Mother #5: "I learned to control my temper. I used the child abuse hotlines, I got counseling early on, and I broke the cycle. Sometimes it helped if I pretended I was being video-taped. Or I would pretend I had just won a million dollars. Or I'd go for a long walk. I stopped yelling and screaming completely."

Mother #6: "We laughed a lot. We looked for the funny side of things and kept a sense of humor no matter what. Life can get pretty serious sometimes, and I think you need to learn how to laugh together."

Mother #7: "The best thing I gave my children was faith in God. We taught them religious principles and gave them a clear sense of God's love for them. We prayed together and gave them spiritual understanding."

Mother #8: "I gave my children time. I decided that ironed clothes and hot meals were nice, but not essential. If we decided to play a game and they missed their baths one day, I didn't feel I had failed. I felt I had finally gotten my priorities straight."

Mother #9: "I let my kids make mistakes. It was the hardest part of parenting, but I held back and let them learn things for themselves. I think they became more independent as a result."

Mother #10: "We let our children know that we expected great things from them. We expected them to come home from dates on time, we expected them to get good grades, we expected them to have good manners. They've told people that they never wondered if we trusted them, and they didn't want to let us down because we believed they could do so much."

Sometimes it's the little things that make children strive to be their best—a kind word of encouragement, an overheard conversation when you brag about a child to a friend, a decision you let them make all by themselves, a heartfelt apology, a shared moment of faith. These are the memories they reflect upon, which motivate and boost them along all their lives. One tiny incident can be a guiding force to them. Aren't there little snatches of conversations that *you* still remember?

Be proud of yourself! Believe in your worth as a good mother. Be good to yourself and enjoy life. Set the example of exuberance, joy, and satisfaction in who you are and what you do.

Know your limits, too. Don't think that you—or anyone else—can completely control a child's destiny. You do your best, and your child still has the freedom to choose his course. Your job is to teach. But your child has a job, too: to learn.

Throw off the guilt that keeps you from enjoying your most fulfilling task: raising children. And always remember that your success does not depend upon theirs. That's the one truth that can make you free—free to be the greatest mom on earth. You can do it—you're doing it right now, in fact. I salute you, and wish you the greatest joy on this marvelous journey.

ABOUT THE AUTHOR

Joni Hilton is the author of numerous novels and nonfiction works specializing in family relationships. She has a Master of Fine Arts degree in professional writing from the University of Southern California, and she writes about parenting for several national magazines. She is also the weekly parenting expert on various radio stations. A former TV talk show host in Los Angeles, she and her husband, Bob, now co-host the syndicated TV show, "Hour Family."

Joni has also instructed parenting classes and worked with inner-city moms to teach them parenting skills. A mother of four children, ages toddler to teen, she offers advice that has been lab-tested right in the trenches.

Next to mothering and writing, Joni enjoys creative cooking, and has entered her award-winning recipes in many state and national cook-offs.